50 SHADES *of* WEALTH

THE
ALLURE
OF
SUCCESS

BARRETT MATTHEWS

Perfect Publishing

ISBN: 978-1-5237-1262-5

TABLE OF CONTENTS

FOREWORD

Webster's Dictionary defines wealth as:

1. much money or property; great amount of worldly possessions; riches

2. the state of having much money or property; affluence: a person of *wealth*

3. a large amount (*of* something); abundance: a *wealth* of ideas

This definition definitely holds true in most circles where material possessions, such as money and tangible riches, equate to success. But in my years on this Earth, I have found that wealth can be defined by the intangible and carry more value than gold. If you follow those we consider wealthy, you will notice that money seems to come rather easily for them. This is because their focus is on things that most of us overlook or ignore.

I was not born wealthy. As a matter of fact, all I had to count on as a child was my sister. We grew up in foster homes and were not as privileged as many of the other children our ages. And, as African American kids growing up in a time where there weren't too many visible wealthy people who looked like us, we were forced to find wealth in other areas. My wealth, and the wealth of those in my circle, centered around relationships. The value in building strong and long relationships cannot be measured and can yield benefits that money cannot buy. They can also build relationships that money can buy. I am sure that you have heard the expression, "It's not what you know, but who you know." Well, as some may see that statement to promote nepotism, it actually supports relationship building.

And what is relationship building? It is nothing more than networking. As Robert Kiyosaki once said, "The richest people in the world look for and build networks. Everyone else looks for a job." Networking is a wealth building strategy that has worked for several successful people, yet is rarely taught as a strategy. Although it is encouraged, networking is rarely shown as a way to create wealth. This may be one of the most unused tools in wealth creation. Hopefully, the lessons and stories you will read in this book will entice you to want to learn "networking" as a business strategy used to create wealth.

My hope is that you will embrace your new relationships and rekindle old ones and use your creativity to forge something strong that will grow and reap benefits for you and those who come in contact with you. Successful people are contacted all of the time by people who need their assistance in a business or personal matters. You may know that many of them are not contacted for their money or riches, but for their contacts, connections and influence. These assets only come from networking and relationship building. It is not something to be taken lightly. Strong relationships that yield results can take years, and even decades to develop. The successful people in this world have put in the time to forge such relationships and have built their dynasties on them. Those on the outside look to get into their world, but don't fully understand the networking that took place to develop such a bond.

50 Shades of Wealth: The Allure of Success is a book that introduces the reader to 10 successful people who have built wealth.

They have built it in the financial arena and the social arena, which makes them all forces in their respective industries. The one takeaway I can share with you, the reader, is that each one of them has really found very little difference between their business life and their personal life. One does not suffer because of the other and one does not exist because of the other. But both are intertwined. The reason these successful people can tie their business and their personal lives together without difficulty is because it all goes back to relationships and networking. Once a bond has been made, the conversation can go almost anywhere and possibilities are endless. As I mentioned earlier, most of the wealthy do not need to talk about money because money comes fairly easy to them. Money is a byproduct of strong business and personal relationships.

When Barrett Matthews decided to write this book, he decided to call upon his own relationships forged through networking with successful people. This book could have easily been called *50 Shades of Success*, because the word "wealth" can sometimes be misleading to some. Although all of the subjects in the book have accumulated their own financial wealth, I think you will find that all of them find more value and success in "who they know" and what those relationships can bring them. The wonderful thing about what Barrett has done is that he has gotten each person to talk about their success; he shows how one can achieve success in many different ways as long as they stay humble, stay determined, constantly work and constantly network. Once you read it, you will notice similarities between yourself and some of the subjects he has interviewed. Realizing this can take you to the place you need to be in order to find your own success. Success and wealth are attainable to all who seek it and are willing and determined to go after it.

So, I urge you to build your own relationships. Forge your own bonds. Rekindle friendships and let God direct your path to your success. Barrett Matthews has done just that and decided to share his relationships with you. This did not happen overnight or by chance. He worked and served, in order to show himself worthy of the time of some of these incredible minds in the business world. Barrett is a worker and a servant and he has dedicated himself to helping others in the best way he knows how. Because of his attitude and his actions, I agreed to lend my name and my words to this book. I ask you to take note of the knowledge that is being shared with you and the message of humility that permeates the chapters from each successful person. This humility is what has led to the relationships that have built the success they have reached and it will be relationships that lead you to your own *50 Shades of Wealth.*

Dr. George C. Fraser
Chairman and CEO of FraserNet, Inc

CHAPTER 1:
NEVER GIVE UP

Myron Golden

 *Myron Golden inspires me. In his best-selling book,* From the Trash Man to the Cash Man: How Anyone Can Get Rich Starting from Anywhere, *Myron describes himself as starting out as a Trash Man. Thankfully, his story changes and eventually he becomes a Cash Man. But not without a lot of hard work along the way.*

Unfortunately, a lot of people start out as the Trash Man. They work hard but can't seem to get ahead. And if they don't do anything about it—if they don't change something—they stay that way. Myron had humble beginnings, in a segregated hospital in Florida where he contracted polio; because of that he's had a leg brace his whole life. Besides that, he grew up poor and didn't know how money worked—at first.

Thankfully, he had parents who taught him well. They taught him to never give up. Even with obstacles, Myron eventually earned a black belt in martial arts. Which goes to show that it doesn't matter where you come from, or what happens to you in life—we all go through something—that doesn't mean you stop trying. In fact, for Myron it meant he tried harder.

Myron remembers the days of barely scraping by, working hard but earning meager wages. He was an actual trash man earning just $6.25 an hour, barely supporting his family. But it was in those years of challenge that he made some of the biggest changes. He read personal development books and prepared to be different.

Later he got into networking marketing on the side, a home-based business. But the process of selling, building a team, and marketing didn't come naturally to him. In fact, it took him a year and half to make his first paycheck. But from Myron we can all learn this important lesson: Never Give Up.

Also the author of Click and Order for Brick and Mortar, *Myron is an integrated marketing consultant who helps businesses and individuals optimize strategies and go for the gold—for many he's helped increase sales to seven and eight figures.*

In his own words, Myron talks about where he came from, and how he became the successful man he is today.

MYRON GOLDEN'S LEARNING CURVE

When I started out, I was probably the worst network marketer in the history of the world. Not only did I not know how to sell, but I also didn't know how to recruit, and I didn't know how to build teams. But I didn't quit because that was the only time in my life I had seen anybody making $10,000 a month.

I lasted through the learning curve.

If I was going to give somebody a success secret that very few people talk about, I would give them the success secret of lasting through the learning curve. If there is something you don't know that you would like to know, no matter what it is—if it's playing the guitar, playing the piano, playing golf, doing construction work—there is going to be a learning curve. And you've got to last through it. One of the biggest causes of failure that I see in the marketplace is people don't last through the learning curve.

THREE FUNCTIONS OF BUSINESS

There are three functions of business:

Innovation
Marketing
Money Management

Innovation means you have to develop, design, create, invent or partner with somebody who has a product that the marketplace is screaming for.

Marketing is the art and science of discovering and developing in other people a desire for more and more of your product and service and opportunity.

Money Management is managing your money so that your outgo doesn't exceed your income, so that your upkeep does not become your downfall.

All three of thee are crucial to being successful and building wealth in your business.

TEAM BUILDING

You also need to build a good team to work with you. What is the biggest hindrance to people in building teams? Probably I would say they are so desperate. The average person is so desperate to build a network marketing team or a direct sales company, they don't build the right kind of team.

They are "needers" instead of leaders. They are very needy and they beg people and try to make it easy for them. Instead of begging people and trying to make it easy for them, if you want to build a huge team and be a powerful recruiter, I can tell you how to do that in two sentences:

1. Be a leader, not a "needer."
2. Instead of making it easy for people, make them qualify for your time.

So that's how I got started, and how I got good at network marketing. I lasted long enough to get good at it. It took me 14 years to get there, and now I am making the hundreds of thousands of dollars a year, making the tens of thousands of dollars a month in that industry. I don't think it has to take anyone 14 years.

BECOMING THE PERSON

Success in business comes from *becoming the person* who can do what will make you successful. Most people don't understand the process, how God set this whole thing up.

God set it up so that we would desire to have a better life. We as human beings were created to be progressively productive. Our entire lives, we are supposed to be getting better. Our life should be getting better. Our work environment should be getting better. Our home environment should be getting better. Our income should be getting better. Our vacations should be getting better. Everything about how we live our lives should be progressively productive.

We desire nice things; there's not a person who doesn't desire a nice car, maybe even a nicer car; a nice home, maybe even a nicer home; a nice vacation or perhaps even a nicer vacation than they're able to take right now. God put that desire to have nice things inside of us. So the desire to have is God-given.

Now, here's what's interesting. God created it so we would become frustrated by our desire to have so that we would be willing to do the thing that is necessary for us to have the things we desire. He made it so that our inability would frustrate us to the point that we would be willing to become the person we needed to be. God's interested in our *becoming*.

We are interested in having. And so he set it up so that we have to do certain things in order to have certain things. But the only way to be able to do those certain things is to grow into the person who can do them. So my biggest challenge in business was becoming the person who could do the thing so I could have the stuff.

The fact is—if you're not successful right now, if you're not achieving the results in your life in any given area, then everything that's going to be necessary for you to achieve success in that area is going to be counter-intuitive to you. The right things are going to feel wrong, and the wrong

"Get out a journal or a notebook and start writing. Make two lists: one will be, 'What Rich People Do,' and one will be 'What Poor People Do.' Start paying attention to the differences between the habits of the rich and the habits of the poor."

Myron Golden
From the Trash Man to the Cash Man

things are going to be right. Think about it. If they felt like the right things to do, you'd already be doing it.

A person is going to have as good a quality life as they are willing to do high quality things. And they are only going to be able to do high quality things if they have become a high quality person.

That's why mentorship and coaching is so essential. Because a coach and a mentor can hold our feet to the fire and assist us in doing those things that are counter-intuitive to us, but actually not counter-productive. Because in doing those things that are counter-intuitive to us so we can experience the results we desire.

TEACHING

Because the network marketing company I was in was in the financial services industry, I learned a lot about how money works early in my life. I learned about the Rule of 72 and how to apply it to my life. So I started teaching other people how to build businesses, how to sell, how to recruit, how to build teams, and how to become leaders. I started also teaching people how money works and how they can make money work for them.

In so doing, I have had the privilege of making millions of dollars in business and teaching other people how to do the same thing. I have students who are making anywhere from a few extra hundred dollars a month, all the way up to people who have used my business strategies to build businesses that make over $10 million a year in revenue.

In 2007, one of my students was on the verge of bankruptcy. But just seven years later, his company did $10.1 million in revenue, in a business that I taught him. That's my greatest success in business, to see my students' success.

I have another student in another country who lost everything. Lost his home, lost his job—everything. I coached him through, and he's built multi-million dollar businesses, he's launched multi-million dollar technology products, in the business world using strategies that I taught him.

Another one of my clients who is in Houston, Texas, wasn't on the verge of bankruptcy. His business was doing ok. But he had to hire 16 new employees and open up a bigger office. He went from doing $12,000 in revenue to doing $80,000 a month in revenue, using the strate-

"When you get into a tight place and everything goes against you, 'til it seems as though you could not hang on a minute longer, never give up then, for that is just the place and time that the tide will turn."

Harriet Beecher Stowe

gies that I taught him. My biggest success in business is also the thing that I get the most joy from, and that is taking my students by the hand and leading them into the financial promised land.

Beyond that, my greatest success is my children working with me. When they were small, they worked with me in my business as employees. Now, having my children work with me side by side in business as we together build their legacy, is probably an even greater success. To know that they will have created their own seven figure fortunes by the time they turn 30 is so exciting to me.

PERSPECTIVE

Without a doubt, the most difficult thing I've ever gone through was when my son died from injuries he sustained in a car accident. That was difficult. That's difficult to this day and there's pain. But because I'm a Christian, and he was a believer in Christ as well, I have peace in my pain. And so, was that a down? Sure, it was a very surreal experience and still is to this day.

In regard to that situation, my biggest personal challenge was becoming the person who is able to go through that situation. It's part of my assignment—becoming the person who can embrace my assignment regardless of what those challenges might be.

There are a lot of challenges we have in our lives that we would not choose. Maybe that's why they are called challenges. They're not called choices. But the challenges in our lives are often the things that make us better people and give us the ability to make better choices going forward.

I understand that as part of my assignment, I don't get to choose which piece I am on God's chess board; I'm just glad that I'm on his chess board. In the end, he's the one who makes the moves. I'm just thankful—if I'm a pawn on his chess board, I thank him for that. If I'm a knight, or a bishop or a rook, or a king, I embrace that. I'm just glad to be a piece on his chess board, whatever my role is to play.

If I was going to tell people how to handle the ups and downs of life and in business, and what are the two keys to living a fulfilled life, I would probably say two things:

1. Figure out what your assignment is. By assignment, I mean why God put you on this Earth. Embrace your assignment, figure out why God put you here, and thank Him for it every day—regardless of what those individual challenges or ups and downs might be.

2. Don't give any energy to outcomes you don't desire in your life. Learn to exchange the anxious apprehension for the outcome you don't desire, for the joyful anticipation of the outcome that you do desire. That will cause you to move towards what you are desiring in life. And it will help you move away from what you don't desire.

MYRON GOLDEN'S FIVE SUCCESS & WEALTH TIPS

1. Read my book, *From the Trash Man to the Cash Man: How Anyone Can Get Rich Starting from Anywhere.*

2. One of the principles in the book is going to lead you to start a business of some kind. There are two types of businesses—one is a business that sells a service, and one in a business that sells a product. I would recommend you start a business that sells a product because it does not limit your time.

3. Read my other book, *Click and Order for Brick and Mortar, Online Strategies for Offline Market Domination.* Once you have a business, that book will teach you how to grow that business.

4. Attend my 1 Year Millionaire Live Workshop. It's a two-day workshop in Tampa, Florida, we host several times a year.

5. Hire me as a consultant, and then I will assist you in accomplishing your financial goals and your business goals. If there is anybody who has any type of business, there is no doubt that I can help them grow their business, three, four, five or 10 fold over what it's doing right now. Visit myrongolden.com for more information.

CHAPTER 2:

LEARN WHAT YOU DON'T KNOW

Tom Schreiter

Tom "Big Al" Schreiter is a man of few words but a man of many talents. Some talents he was born with, and others he learned along the way over many years of trial and error. As an engineer, he seemed an unlikely network marketer. But something inside him was burning to get free.

Free of everything that a typical 9-5 job entails. And financially free. Free to be his own boss.

The thing about Big Al that impresses me the most is his willingness to change. Sometimes we want something different in our lives, but we want to keep on staying the same people we always have been. It doesn't work that way, and Big Al is living proof. He knew right off the bat that as he changed his profession, he'd need to learn new skills and change as a person.

Though he didn't learn it all at first, he was open and willing to learn. So when a chance to change came along, he was ready. Are you?

In his own words, Big Al talks about transformation, and how sometimes it doesn't happen the way we think it will.

TOM SCHREITER ON FINDING A BETTER LIFE

In 43 years of trial and error, all I've done is kept track of what works and doesn't work.

I was an engineer. Like a lot of people, I wanted to earn more money, especially when our jobs don't pay very much. So I just answered an ad looking for an opportunity. I was already sold on doing something when I answered the ad. I didn't really need a presentation, I just needed somebody to listen and point me in the right direction.

I was incompetent. I had studied to be an engineer, and so I knew nothing about business. I knew nothing about people. I always say engineers are shy, personality-free, charisma bypass, socially challenged, should not be let out in public people, and that was me. At the time, I decided to take my engineering mathematics skills and do network marketing. You can see that train wreck waiting to happen. That was my biggest struggle.

> "Education is what remains after one has forgotten what one has learned in school."
>
> **Albert Einstein**

The problem is, when things aren't working, we don't know how to fix them. Because if we did, we would have them fixed. And if we don't know what we don't know, it's almost impossible for us to learn what we don't know—because we don't know what we don't know. So then we end up knowing stuff we don't need to know, and it's just a black hole.

Unless somebody else takes you out of that black hole, you're going to be there forever, because you don't even know what direction to go in or how to get out of there. So that is what happened to me in 1974. I didn't learn a new set of skills for a new profession. At first.

My struggle was, I was spending a lot of time and not earning any money, and that was just stupid to everybody on the outside. I was just using brutal hard work and effort, repeating bad skills over and over. I guess that is the definition of insanity. My strategy was to just keep doing the same thing, even though it didn't produce results, because I didn't know where I could find out how to do it better.

BUSINESS IS ABOUT PEOPLE

Somebody who knew more than me said, "Hey, why don't you look at it this way?" And then things turned around.

Over time, I did learn what to say and do. The big secret is— business is about people, not about products and services. Products and services don't sell themselves. They don't have legs. My biggest accomplishment is learning about people. People move products. People move services. People move messages. They don't move themselves, so we have to learn the skills of getting this information inside of people's minds so they can make a decision and say, "Hey, this might be useful for me."

I learned what words and phrases worked to get our message across and what words and phrases don't work. Then out of the words and phrases that did work, I'd say, let's take the ones that work almost all the time.

People hate rejection. All we want to do is have people hear our message. And then they can decide if it's for them or not. Our biggest struggle is, we don't know how to get people to hear our message.

Our message bounces off the front of their heads and tinkles to the floor because it's blocked by so many things people think:

> "The difference between winning and losing is most often not quitting."
>
> **Walt Disney**

- The sales alarm.
- The too-good-to-be-true filter.
- The what's-the-catch filter.
- I should be skeptical.
- Are you a salesman?
- Are you trying to take my money?

Until we learned how to get past all that garbage, our message would never go inside their heads. And then we are effectively withholding our message from them and that's almost criminal. You have something they need. All we want to do is get the message in their head, because this will fix their need. It's up to them whether they want to do it or not. But we have to get past all that garbage.

My biggest success was finally making an income from all my effort.

TOM SCHREITER'S FIVE SUCCESS & WEALTH TIPS

1. If you're going to take on a new profession, learn a new set of skills.

2. If you want to make the money right away, and get on with life and do what you want, learn the skills right away. Life ain't forever!

3. Having a team is always better than just being by yourself, because you can only affect so many people. We can only see so many people. We are limited in hours in a day. Build a team.

4. When you're learning skills, just keep everything in perspective. It's not the technical skills that count, it's the people skills that count.

5. When you're building a team, it's all about building leaders, not individual people. So concentrate your effort on the few people that share your vision and want to go in the same direction.

CHAPTER 3:
DREAM BIG

Dr. Willie Jolley

Do what you love. That's something I believe in, and it's one reason why I love Dr. Willie Jolley's story. He actually found something he didn't know he loved until it discovered him. That happens sometimes; we started out doing one thing, but then we realize our potential in another field.

Once he found this thing, which for him was public speaking combined with music and a message, he made it his life. He dreamed big and didn't take no for an answer. Are there challenges along the way? Of course. But that doesn't stop Willie from dreaming, making goals, and then doing everything in his power to achieve that dream.

Life takes us in funny directions sometimes, but usually it's for a reason. A better reason than we will ever imagine. Read about Willie's experience in his own words.

DR. WILLIE JOLLEY'S COURSE CORRECTION

I was a singer and an entertainer making my living in the entertainment and music business. Once I got married I wanted be home more, so I started a night club back in the Washington, D.C., area. I built it into one of the top night spots in DC; it became very popular. But one night I went in, and they said, "We've made a change; we love your band and love what you've done, but there's a cheaper way to get a full club. So we bought a karaoke machine."

I was devastated. I said, "Well what about my bills?" And I realized no one really cares about your bills but the people you owe. It was in that moment that I decided it was time for me to do something else. I was trying to figure out what I was going to do with myself.

So I took a job with the Washington, D.C., public school system. In that job I started giving little speeches to kids. As part of that I learned something about myself I did not know—that I could do something other than sing to communicate.

As I was speaking to kids and teachers, and then their associations, they'd invite me to their churches. Then someone at their church would invite me to their company. It continued to grow. At one point, Les Brown heard about me—that I was speaking and singing and putting it altogether. He invited me to be on tour with him and Gladys Knight as part of the music and motivation dream team tour. That allowed me to meet new people who I would never have met.

Then I got a little radio show, and it just continued to grow. From there the books came, and one thing led to another. But it all started with me finding something that I loved and finding something that I could do. When I found it, or rather it found me, I just continued to pursue it and continued to make a commitment to get better and better.

Someone asked me recently, "Do you ever go to amusement parks? Do you go to amusement parks and get on a roller coaster?"

I said, "No, I don't go to amusement parks or roller coasters. I don't need a roller coaster, I'm an entrepreneur." An entrepreneur by his nature is up and down. It's a roller coaster. It's a constant up and down; it's always challenging.

> "So many of our dreams at first seem impossible, then they seem improbable, and then, when we summon the will, they soon become inevitable."
>
> **Christopher Reeve**

BUSINESS IS LIKE SCHOOL

Business is like school; it's a challenge at every stage. When you were in first grade, what was your biggest challenge? Learning your ABCs and basic reading. If you wouldn't have learned that, you wouldn't have been able to go to grade 2. So, at that point that was the biggest challenge you had. But next, when you got to grade 2, you had to put all those things into more complex sentences, or in math you also might have learned how to do subtraction and division. So then if you can't learn all that, then you can't get to the next grades. It's just like that in business.

In business, in every level there's a challenge. The biggest challenge is the first big one. For me, my first big one was the first summer I was in business—I needed to pay my bills. But I was only speaking to schools, and schools let out in the summer. How was I going to pay my bills those three months? I had to hustle and just beat the bushes until I was able to get two little contracts—one with a summer camp, and the other one with an art school to speak for that summer. Somehow I survived. I made $2,700 that summer. That was my biggest challenge at the time.

But, once I faced that challenge and overcame it, then the next big challenge was like—phhh! Now, I might have a deal now that might be facing me that might be $3 million. So there are challenges at every level, but that first big challenge is the hardest.

There's a great story about this old servant who had a dream one night that he saw the face of death. So he got on his fastest horse. To his master he said, "I've got to out run the face of death." He rode his horse for three days without stopping. Finally came to a place where there was a fork in the road. He wasn't sure which way to go, so he tried both.

> "From a great minute comes a great hour, and from a great hour comes a great day and from a great day comes a great week, and then a great month, then a great year, and from there you can be the architect of a great lifetime and it starts with a single minute!"
>
> **Dr. Willie Jolley**
> *It Only Takes a Minute to Change Your Life*

He'd go on one side for a while, then he'd for the other side; he'd ride over, and back and forth, back and forth. All the while, he was trying to out run the face of death. About a mile down the road, the face of death appeared and said, "Omar, why have you been keeping me waiting?"

The lesson is that you can twist and you can turn and you can run and you can hide, but you can't get out of loss. It's not possible.

You're going to have some stuff that happens. You just deal with it and go forward understanding that there will be some setbacks, there will be some challenges, but it really comes down to this: dream, believe, take action, commit, and have the faith to keep fighting.

REACHING SUCCESS LITTLE BY LITTLE

I transform people's thinking so they can transform their futures. It is a great business to be in.

Staying open for 24 years is a big accomplishment. Most businesses don't survive one year or five years, and 10 is just amazing. So to be able to keep the lights on, not have another job for 24 years except speaking, is amazing. How do we do it? We just gotta keep hustling.

I've been named one of the top 5 speakers of the world, I've been named Motivational Speaker of the Year, I've been named top 10 speaker by eSpeaker, top 5 leadership speakers, I've had best-selling books, television and radio, I just replaced Zig Ziglar on the national motivation tour. But all of those are just continuing to just do what you do and do it well.

I helped Ford with their turnaround. They were on the brink of bankruptcy. As a speaker, they brought me in to help. I helped to transform their thinking. I worked with them for a few years. In 2009, Ford was the only one of the three big auto makers that was able to reject the government bailout and go on to billion dollar profits.

I've worked with companies, organizations, and individual people who have bought my books: *It Only Takes a Minute to Change Your Life*, and bestseller *A Setback is a Setup for Comeback*. They are all part of what you build in your body of work. I'm very grateful and blessed to have some accomplishments that go with the fact that it seems to be working, because so many people around the globe now have been saying, "This guy has impacted my life," which was why I started doing it.

RELYING ON FAITH

In 2003, I lost my mother, my brother and my father-in-law all within 30 days. How do you get through those times? Everyone will experience personal devastation. It can crush you and it can kill your business and it can kill your life. That's where your faith comes in.

The way I got through that was by the grace of God, and it's been an amazing experience. (Read more about it in *Chicken Soup for the Christian Soul II.*) The biggest thing is that there will be some new challenge around the corner. How will you face it? It's about the mindset.

Success is not just about financial success because then there are the other parts of life—family, marriage, business relationships. There's so much other beyond just making money that it is amazing. My biggest accomplishment is my marriage to my wife. I married really, really well. We recently celebrated 30 years of marriage. We are blessed. It's work! All of that is work. Believe me, everything takes work.

My faith is singularly connected. My faith in God impacts every part of my life. I'm not out there to make anyone else believe the way I believe. But here's what's worked for me. Faith has sustained me in every facet of my life.

DR. WILLIE JOLLEY'S FIVE SUCCESS & WEALTH TIPS

1. You must dream big dreams. You really do have to dream.

2. Start working on your belief system. Work on your belief system just like you work on your muscles at a gym. Start with a 5-pound weight, then 10-pound weight then 20-pound weight; just the same you have to work on your belief system. You have to believe that it is—and if you don't believe it is, then you will never have thought to do the things necessary. The challenges, the setbacks, the situations, circumstances, the issues of life will beat you down and you'll say, "Well, I just give up." When you've been told all your life that your dreams aren't possible or that you can't do anything, then to dream big is really hard. You have to believe that those dreams are possible. So work on your belief system.

3. Sit down and write out your goals. Everybody has heard somewhere in their life, you need to set goals. But only a few people out of a hundred set goals. Why? Because it's hard. Les Brown said, "Most people are seriously not serious." It takes work. It's cognitive conscious effort.

4. You must act on those beliefs and those dreams. You've got to take an action step. And again, that's hard. Because there are going to be some challenges.

5. Make a commitment to finish the journey. Commit yourself to that journey. Once you get committed, you have to commit to your commitment, because there's going to be something that's going to test you. It's going to happen. Not maybe. Life is going to test you. It's waiting for you.

CHAPTER 4:
MIND SHIFT

Amed Hazel

 *Amed Hazel has had a lot of ups and downs in life. And at some point, we all will, too. We can't stop them from happening, because even in our best times, they happen. So instead of asking why they happen, let's ask, what can we do about them?*

For Amed, in his year of continual downs, he made a decision. Instead of reacting, he was going to act. After all the downs, he was going to make a mind shift. He was going to look at what was most important in his life and then change.

Change isn't easy, but it's necessary. If we want our lives to be great, then we must change how we think and then change how we act. That is when our lives will begin to change for the better. Read in his own words how he was able to make a mind shift and what happened as a result.

AMED HAZEL LEARNS THE HARD WAY

The market was crazy in Baltimore, Maryland. It was an insider's market. My wife and I didn't really understand that at the time, so we backed away from it. Around 2007 we started investigating in it heavy again, and dove into the market and started wholesaling real estate properties. We took a course, and it was just the right time for us.

But we quickly realized it was difficult on us time-wise. We had a time management problem. We talked business 24 hours a day. There were times when we would have the computer and the printer in the bed in between us. The printer was running all night long! We were printing up marketing materials. Literally, at a point the business came between us. We were at each other's throats.

At the time, we were running to appointment after appointment. We are making money, but the machine that we were running was consuming money just as fast. So I was helping people making money, I was connecting the dots, but I didn't actually know how to make money off of what I was doing. There were times that I was doing multi-million dollar deals, but I wasn't making money because I didn't understand how to. We were making really good money but we were spending a lot of it. We were leaving the kids with babysitters and it was consuming us heavily.

The biggest struggle that we faced was managing capital and understanding where capital comes from. We were making a lot of money but we were spending a lot of money

"Do not dwell in the past, do not dream of the future, concentrate the mind on the present moment."

Buddha

senselessly. We were bidding deals and doing deals, but we weren't including the cost of gas, marketing materials, and marketing systems. We were bidding deals competitively but we just weren't keeping track of the finances like we should have been.

THE YEAR OF CHANGE

In July 2008, we lost our 19 year old son to a heart attack. Then in August my aunt passed away, in September my niece passed away, and then in October my cousin passed away. In November my mother went into the hospital with blood clots on her lungs, and it looked like she wasn't going to make it. She did. She's well and fine today but it was just too much in 2008.

During that time, my wife and I also ran a full-time brick and mortar martial arts school. So we were running two full-time businesses. We had to do real estate during the daytime and on the weekends, but Monday through Saturday during mornings and evenings, we taught martial arts. And we were raising our kids.

So in November, the martial arts school was going well, but one night after class I looked at my wife and I said, "We're closed."

She said, "I know, I'm getting the books together and we're wrapping it up now."

I touched her on the shoulder and I said, "No, we're closed."

She asked, "What do you mean?"

I said, "I'm done." And she really stopped and really looked at me deeply and I said, "I'm done, baby."

She said, "Well, what do we do?"

I said, "Pack up this stuff, whatever we can carry, put in the back of our Tahoe and we're closing the school."

We went from teaching a full entire class, exhausted, tired, at 10 p.m., looking to go home, we hadn't eaten dinner, and we just loaded the truck up. We got done about 2 a.m. and we never went back.

The thing was, we took all that stuff back to our home and loaded our home with that stuff. We went from having a well-kept house to junk and stuff everywhere. We started doing demo projects in the house, and we had a semi-flood in the house, so there was drywall and dust everywhere. It looked like a construction zone.

During all of that time, we had life happening to us and we stopped cleaning. We went from having a very well-kept and clean house to a very dirty and disorganized house. We divorced ourselves from our home.

For us, it was a mind shift that 2008 hit us and broke us. And it was a mind shift to make us understand, investigate how money works and investigate how we needed to manage our time and investigate what was important to us. It was that mind shift, where we thought, "Wait a minute. We're doing this all wrong." We're doing this all wrong. Because we understand how to make $30-50,000 in a month, but it's killing us. The money is there to be made. But how do you do it and not have it kill you?

That year was agonizing. It got to the point where my wife and I thought as a couple, we were not going to make it, or that the family was not going to make it. We hit a breaking point. So we shifted. We shifted from wholesaling real estate to investing in distressed assets. It changed our lives.

WHAT COMES FIRST

When we actually got started in the business, we were looking at making a shift from this difficult situation in our lives to a more successful situation. My wife and I, neither one of us was actually working a job. So when I made the shift, I went from working a lot, being a workaholic and not really seeing family, to falling deeper in love with family. What happened is kind of like a slingshot.

My biggest personal life accomplishment goes back to that mind shift and learning that the love of family is the ultimate thing. It is the ultimate thing. You may hear it, but having a deep awareness of love and how to give it and how to receive it—a lot of times we don't even know how to receive love. So understanding that is one of the keys that actually made me stronger in business. To love my family and understand what that means.

If my wife or son are with me in a meeting, and they need to leave in the middle of that meeting, I will stop the meeting. I will kiss my wife, hug my son, and tell them that I'll see them later. Because they are most important.

Now we invest in distressed mortgages. That is people who have not been able to pay their mortgage due to an apparent economic crisis and most importantly due to the 2008 economic crisis. When people cannot pay, we go to the banks and buy those mortgages at

> "The key is not to prioritize what's on your schedule, but to schedule your priorities."
>
> **Stephen Covey**

a reduced rate. Then, we call the people up and we talk with them; we don't do it personally, but we have different systems and we seek out a solution for those people. We get people re-performing on their mortgages, and we work with them in a kind manner.

We understand what it is like to have hard times. Even though we were making money, we were still having hard times. We understand that good people run into difficult situations. We talked to people on the phone and would say, "We're not a bank. We're not going to talk to you mean and nasty, but we'd like to get you to work with us and get back on track. That's extremely profitable for you."

When I was back in business again, I didn't know how to make money in this industry because I didn't have a coach. I didn't have anyone to talk to, and this industry was brand new. It was a brand newborn baby. And the entire country didn't really know what to do inside of this industry. So over time I developed a reputation for being a connector.

I had banks and buyers contacting me, and once I learned how to make money, instead of tens of thousands of dollars flowing into our bank account, we started looking at millions flowing into our bank account. Self taught.

AMED HAZEL'S FIVE SUCCESS & WEALTH TIPS

1. **Be patient with yourself.** Whatever you're studying, whatever your endeavor is, be patient with yourself. You can study a course, you can get a college degree, you can try to do whatever, but you have to be patient. Sometimes it may take you 5-10 years to become successful in your field. So you have be patient with yourself and not buy into the concept of, "Hey I did it in 12 months!" For me, it was a long process of discovering me and who I am that actually contributed to that shift in 2008.

   In ancient Egypt when people were inducted into their mystery schools, they had to go through an arduous process that could last 20-40 years before they allowed them in. All of the scholars we look at today like Pythagoras, Aristotle and Socrates were all failures. They never made it into the Egyptian mystery system. They flunked out and were sent back to their respective countries. Be patient with yourself.

2. **Keep what's first *first*.** For me that is family. Putting family first is one of the gems that I got from it. It took me from failure to success. Once I had and understood that love of family, I became more relaxed.

   Then, I understood on a deeper level that when I went to someone's house to evaluate their current situation as far as real estate was concerned, instead of thinking, "Oh yeah this is going to be a good deal here!" We were looking at it differently. "This is a family. These people are having a hard time."

There would be sometimes that we would listen to someone's story sitting in their living room crying with them. We were thinking, wow, this is a serious situation. Sometimes we had to tell the homeowner, "We can't help you because we can't make money off you at your further detriment."

3. **No matter what, life is going to happen.** If you're looking at your situation and think, "Oh my God, this came and hit me and knocked me down." Jerry D. Clark talks about Murphy's Committee; it's not just Murphy's Law, but it's a committee! You'll have successive hits. You will have this happening and that happening.

Things were looking better for us in 2009, but then someone broke into our house and took everything. And then again someone broke into our house the next year. Life will happen to you! While you are going through your transformation. Life doesn't care about you being down. You have to know how to maintain it. Again, we were making money but we were still going through difficult times. Life is going to happen to you while you're on your journey. How you handle it is going to determine if Murphy's Committee continues to beat you down.

4. **Read all the books.** During your study of your particular field, you have to become well read. You have to have a knowledge and understanding of business and finance and how it all works. You have to understand that your knowledge comes in what you know technically, but it also comes in your internal and external communication. What people are saying to you, what you are saying to yourself, and what you know about your business. But all of that can be re-directed when you are reading books in your particular field.

Knowing the ins and outs of what you are doing, personal development, mindset training—you have to read the books to acquire that knowledge.

5. **Call people.** Find out who the players are in your field and pick up the phone and call them, or email them. Visit their website, get on their mailing list and find out if you can have lunch. I have an extremely hectic schedule, but if someone reaches out to me—the first, second, third, or fourth time they reach out to me, they may not get me. But if you are persistent I'll say, "Wait a minute! Who is this guy or girl who is constantly trying to get me? Buy me lunch and I will talk to you." During that time you'll wind up getting a lot of information out of me.

CHAPTER 5:
THE SERIAL ENTREPRENEUR

Jasmine O'Day

Jasmine O'Day not only achieved success, but she achieved it against the odds. As a single mom, it wasn't easy for her to work, let alone be an entrepreneur. She is living proof that anyone, at any stage of their life, can be their own boss.

But as she also experienced, you can work and work and become successful, and then lose it all. Even that didn't stop her. She picked up the pieces and started over. This time, she started her own businesses, and she invested in multiple businesses. In her own words, read about how she diversifies in order to have the life she wants.

JASMINE O'DAY ON GOING FROM HOMELESS TO MILLIONAIRE

My beginnings were very different. I really didn't have the notion to work for someone else. As a little girl I always said I was going to be the boss of something. I wasn't sure what. But I knew I wanted to be the boss of something.

Later, I was working and I needed to supplement my income. I started working for a vending machine company. Just a guy who owned a couple routes of vending machines and he needed some help. I saw it and I went into it. I learned so much about it. I was pretty innovative and he didn't have to manage me. To make a long story short, I did so well that when he took ill and could not run the business, I was the head of the business.

Later on, I talked to my father, telling him that I wasn't happy with corporate America; I wasn't happy with working for other people. I had children at a young age and I wanted to give them a certain type of life. We talked about exploring entrepreneur opportunities.

I was able to purchase businesses like a nightclub and go into the liquor business with him and sell the vending machine company. Later on in life, I acquired ATMs and vending machines and went into the car wash business with my dad. It became quite addictive for me, because back then it didn't cost a whole heck of a lot to invest in those things. Sure, I've made some mistakes along the way. I've lost money, and I've gained money. But I always wanted to have the freedom.

My biggest struggle in my personal life was when I was homeless. Who would have thought that by the age of 30 and I was worth a few million, and I would lose it several years later and be homeless in the back of a vehicle and have to start literally all over?

I didn't let myself down. It was very important for me to continue to set the path for financial freedom so I just never gave up. It was never an option to give up and failure was never an option. You don't allow anybody to dictate your salary ceiling. You control your economy. You control your wealth, and you control your poverty. You can control your fear.

When your fear wants to overtake you, and you make excuses that you have no money to do this, you have no money to do this or that—I want you to go back to this chapter and read. Read about the part where I was homeless, and my bank account was wiped out. I had nothing left but boxes. I had sold our furniture on Craigslist; you name it, I was getting rid of it and I was selling it to survive. I was trying to hold onto that house as long as I could. When I couldn't do it anymore, it was time to go. I got evicted. I put what I had in storage, I packed suitcases and put them in the trunk with a cooler, and that is what we did until we could go get something else.

So then I started a cleaning company for under $70, and it took time. To start a blue collar business that I knew nothing about was a struggle. But I did it because at that point, it was about survival. I went from being financially free, to having nothing and having to survive. So the natural instincts, my animalistic instincts like a lioness, kicked in because my children depended on me. Survival kicked in and nothing was going to stop me from being able to provide.

> "A dreamer is one who can only find his way by moonlight, and his punishment is that he sees the dawn before the rest of the world."
>
> **Oscar Wilde**

Once I got out of survival mode—once my company was thriving—I didn't really have a plan of action. I just knew I wanted to make money to get out of that homeless situation and be able to get into a place and be able to feed my kids and things like that. Once I got past that, and once it really started, I never stopped. I kept doing it.

It all starts with the mindset. I grew the business to $9 million. That should be inspirational for you to know that you have to control your bank account, your salary, your outcome. The mindset should be, I am better than being somebody's employee for the rest of my life. If you want to be somebody's employee, that's fine, but you should also have other things going on that compensate and make up that income that you're not receiving.

Once it started thriving, I realized I could go back into being a serial entrepreneur. Having multiple streams of revenue in case I didn't get that big city contract, just in case I didn't get that airport contract, just in case this month this client was late. I had many months where clients were late. They didn't pay at 30 days; they may have paid at 45 or they may have paid at 50, but I was depending on that money. Once I got past that struggle, I had other streams that would pick up the slack for whatever was lacking. What started happening was it was an influx, constantly, of money coming from every company that I was involved in.

That's when I soared.

FINALLY LETTING GO

I worked for a company at the same time that I was running these businesses. I was very comfortable with the paycheck. It was secure; I knew it was always going to be paid every two weeks. I wasn't ready to give that up. Believe it or not, I was a little fearful to give that up. One day my position was taken away from me, and I didn't have a choice.

I took away a nice severance and I realized then that I had exactly what I wanted, which was financial freedom. I didn't realize that was exactly what I was seeking. I didn't just want to be a boss in something and be something, but I actually wanted financial freedom. I realized then that's what I had. I worked so hard in my teens and 20s and early 30s; I finally had acquired financial freedom. So that was the start of where I am now. I realized on that path, it was really financial freedom that I wanted.

My biggest struggle in business was a time that I was trying to find balance. I had so many things that I wanted to do that I felt like I was supposed to balance like a gymnast or a ballerina. But that was not the case at all. There is no such thing as balance. What you have to do is put 100% into whatever you're doing at that time. I'd heard so many things: focus on one thing, don't do multiple things, you can't make multiple things happen. The truth was, I had to do what worked for me.

I've always been a scatterbrained entrepreneur. I've always come up with ideas in the wee hours of the morning and I'd run with them. I want to do so much. How do I do all this, and balance? My struggle was trying to balance. I drove myself crazy trying to find balance. Well, there's no such thing as balance.

I had to build teams. My struggle at the time was that I had so much passion, I had to find people who had the same passion or were knowledgeable or even some that were more knowledgeable so I didn't have to micromanage.

In the beginning you say, money's an issue. But I can't use money as an excuse because if money was an excuse, nobody would be an entrepreneur. Most entrepreneurs either start with no money or very little money, and some were homeless like myself. I realized I had to put one foot in front of the other and stay focused on whatever I was doing at that particular time, and it would come to fruition. Whatever I wanted to happen would happen. Whatever strategies I was implanting would implement.

There was a time where I trusted everyone; I was very naïve with people who were shady and people who were stealing. I was very naïve because I wasn't that type of person, so I didn't see that in other people. Whatever they were telling me was exactly what I wanted, so I had no problem writing the check.

So then trust became a big struggle for me. I had lost a lot of money. Business people in my life would tell me one thing, and that they could do this for me and I'd pay them thousands of dollars, and they didn't come through with it. I had to learn that in business I could not trust anybody.

Later on I became very smart. I would say, "If you want to do this, then this is what we need to do first." I would make them work for that check. They would have to show me some things for that check.

I had some businesses fail because I refused to hire somebody on to do something and I did it myself. Years later I started those businesses back up, and they thrived because I had more education. So the more education, the more knowledge and networking with the right people, will help you grow. All those struggles began to subside and go out the window until the struggling companies that I did have became successful.

Unfortunately, along the way my relationships suffered. I lost a lot of people in my life. I was a single mom, and so I wanted to make sure that I maintained a relationship with my children while I was building what I call an empire. I didn't want to neglect them in the process. There were some things that I sacrificed both in my personal life and in business to make sure that I could still spend time with my sons and have a good relationship and upbringing with my sons while building the company.

ADDING VALUE, BEING AN ASSET

My father always said, add value to someone's life. I always want to add value, I always want to be that person and to be of value. Because if I don't add value, that means I'm a liability and I never want to be a liability. I always want to add value and be an asset in someone's life. And so that has been a major personal accomplishment that I'm an asset as a mother, I'm an asset as a friend, I'm an asset as a coach, I'm an asset as a consultant. Every last one of my clients that I coach, whether they started off slow or not, they are on the exact path they wanted to be on. Because you win some and you lose some.

My biggest accomplishment in my businesses is that I have control. I can actually invest in other businesses. I don't have to ask banks for money, I don't have to rely on other people's money, although I do have partners in other businesses I don't have to do that. I don't owe anybody any money and I have complete control financially.

To be able to have your own resources and fund your own businesses and projects is great. When people come to my investment group, I'm able to make a decision whether

> "I'm a dreamer. I have to dream and reach for the stars, and if I miss a star then I grab a handful of clouds."
>
> **Mike Tyson**

to invest in their business or not. That's an accomplishment to me. I never thought I'd be here. That's not something I used to fathom when I was little, and to see it now it's just amazing. It feels surreal.

I have raised free-thinking sons who have followed in the path of being financially responsible, have used their jobs as resources to start their own businesses; even my 10-year-old has an entrepreneurial spirit. Being able to finally have a personal life is an accomplishment.

Believe it or not, I guess there was a part of me that wanted to prove something to those that have doubted me, and I've done that. I know that that sounds crazy, and it may sound a little vain and it may sound a little cocky, but when you have people all your life telling you that you can't do this, or you can't do that, or you've been bullied, then it feels good to accomplish what you set out to do.

So when you've had people talk about you, and to finally be where I am now, that is an accomplishment. To have great relationships with my children and to teach them what I know about wealth and financial freedom, and when they have off-spring, they will never want for anything. That is a major accomplishment, to have a special someone in my life, and that finally gets it and now he's an entrepreneurial path and I'm helping him on his path.

You're only as good as your clients. Your client has to want it. You can't want it more than them. You just can't. An accomplishment for me was when I pulled someone under my wing to teach them what I knew. When they left me, whether they left early or they left late, they left me knowing more than they knew when they came in.

The major connection to all of this is trust. Trust is a major thing that you have to have in both your personal and in your business. Being able to focus on both your personal life and your business life. Those are major connections. Having discipline. You know, I was disciplined financially; I didn't have any major expenses that were just frivolous to me. There was a time that I had no cable, I didn't get my nails done professionally, I didn't get my hair done professionally, I didn't go out, I didn't have a car payment. Because what I wanted was more important. I was really disciplined financially. Because I felt like I knew later it would pay off. And it did.

I was also doing a lot of self development. I was learning who I was, learning more about me on a day to day basis, and allowing people to pour into my ear —General Napoleon Hill, Les Brown—just people that poured into me and my spirit about business life the power of the subconscious mind, the law of attraction. That's very important in my personal life and my business life because without clarity, you have chaos. And with chaos, you can't produce cash.

Also, without clarity, you can't have a successful family, and you can't have a successful business. So there has to be clarity so there's no chaos so that you can produce the positive and possible fruits in your life, business, family, and you just can't have it without that. So those things all come together in both personal and business.

BENEFITS OF MULTIPLE COMPANIES

One thing about me being a serial entrepreneur is that I know I will never ever be in poverty again. It is very important to understand that nobody can dictate my paycheck but me. I don't punch anybody's clock but my own. Nobody can tell me I have reached a salary ceiling, a salary cap of $200,000-3,000,000 a year. No one can tell me when to go on vacation, no one can tell me when to go on break.

It is an amazing feeling to be an entrepreneur and even more so to be a serial entrepreneur. Because you know everything that you touch, every business that you're involved in, it's producing fruit, it's producing revenue. You can sit back and make money in your sleep. I have a revenue stream that when I wake up in the morning I check the bank account, and maybe there has been $3,000 of this type of purchase or whatever the case may be. That's a good feeling.

I've had the opportunity to build not one but four companies that are worth over a million dollars in a short period of time, and they all started with very little money. They grew because word of mouth or the type of business.

In our luxury travel concierge company, there is not one travel deal that we do for less than $15,000. We sold two islands last year and four jets in the first four months of us opening up the opportunity of selling jets and islands. To have the freedom to build these connections with jet companies and boutique hotels, and things like that, that is an accomplishment because that was a field that I knew nothing about. I went in because travel has always been always been my passion. I've always been connected with some pretty great people, and I just took a chance. It worked.

I'm also in the cannabis industry. I'm in Denver, Washington state, California, Arizona, Las Vegas, and Oregon. Within the first quarter, we had generated close to a half a million dollars. So that is a business that is not going anywhere.

I have a health company now. I have books that are coming out. I have a coaching business, a consulting business, and an investment firm; I do real estate investing. All of these things. And then I'm involved in over 30 businesses with people that have brought me in as an investor or on the board of directors;

in those I have a percentage and control over what they do and how they produce and market and control over their earnings. That is an amazing feeling.

It is powerful and empowering to help someone increase their revenue and their company and their employees. They're providing jobs. It's an amazing feeling. If anyone tells you that being a serial entrepreneur is just something that people talk about, they have no idea. There are so many different things you can do.

It's very important to understand that your job is not secure. No job is secure. Not even the president. If they want you out, they will get you out. Please understand that. To have multiple streams of revenue besides that job is showing responsibility. Because if you get that pink slip tomorrow and you don't have multiple streams of revenue producing, how are you going to pay your mortgage? How are you going to pay that car payment? How are you going to pay your bills and how are you going to feed your family?

I love to help people make money. I've had clients who say, "Jasmine, in six months I want to fire my boss."

I say, "Ok let's sit down and talk about that. What are you making now? What are you trying to do?" I created a strategy so that they can do that.

JASMINE O'DAY'S FIVE SUCCESS & WEALTH TIPS

1. **Surround yourself with people that you would like to be like.** These are people who have already traveled that path, who are more successful than you and who know more than you. Look at your circle of five. Does your circle of five encourage you? Do they push you? Can they get you help you get to where you want to be? If they don't, then you need to change your circle.

    How do you meet these people? You have to go to events that cultivate you and produce that seed of growth. So if you want to start in real estate, then start going to these events that help you learn about real estate. If you want to be an investor, then you have to start learning about that. If you want to get into stocks, or if you want to get into cannabis, then learn about those industries. Whatever industry you're trying to get in or whatever you're trying to do, surround yourself by those people and start going to those types of events.

2. **You have to read.** Turn the TV off for a little bit and read. Pick up a book. Pick up a success book. Read *The Alchemist*, read *The Four Agreements*, read *The Spiritual Law*, read *Rich Dad, Poor Dad*, Read, read, read, read, read! *The Power of Now*, *The Power of Influencing People*. Start reading.

3. **You need to meditate.** Set aside time to clear your mind. Think about where you want to be in your life. Start really connecting with your higher self. Remove all the negative energy in your life so that positive things can flow in. A lot of times we're on social media and things like that, and a lot of negativity can stream in. You need to meditate and clear your mind so that throughout your day, you can conquer whatever task you're trying to conquer. Make sure the things you want to do, you can do.

4. **Set goals.** A lot of people don't write down their goals. You need to set daily goals and monthly goals. You need to set short term goals and long term goals. Write the vision, and make a claim. The reason that you're writing down the vision is once you put things down on paper, it becomes law. You have to look at it, and you have marinate on it. You have to meditate on it.

Now you have to figure out how to accomplish these goals. Don't think about and don't be afraid. Just do it! Everything you want to accomplish, just do it. Don't let anybody tell you what you cannot do. They're not you; as a matter of fact, that should be your fuel to push forward. One thing about me is, if you tell me I can't do it, I'm gonna do it harder because I'm going to tell you that you don't know what you're talking about. I'm going to make it happen because you just told me that I couldn't.

Just do it. Don't think about the outside negative people. Don't think about yourself, because you are your worst critic and you hold yourself back. Just do it. And if you surround yourself with positive people they're going to push you to do it because they're not going to let you stop. Do it.

5. **Invest in yourself.** Invest in the necessary things, whether it's coaching, books, materials, digital materials, or seminars, you have to invest. If you really want to be wealthy, you have to invest; it's not going to just fall in your lap. You even have to pay to play the lotto. So even with windfall comes a little bit of investment.

CHAPTER 6:
WRITE YOUR FUTURE

Kym Yancey

Kym Yancey is one of the best creative minds I know. He's also not afraid to try new things and forge new paths. That is one thing you have to do to be successful and build wealth. You have to be willing to take that step and take a risk. Sometimes things work out, and sometimes they don't. But at least be willing to try.

What Kym started out doing in his career was pretty far removed from where he is now, but each job or business along the way is a learning experience. It's how he gears up for the next best thing. While you are out there in each new business venture, be open to what it can teach you. It will be a valuable experience you can always take with you.

Read in Kym's own words how he grew over the years, had opportunities to grow, and now has a rewarding business with his wife of 38 years.

KYM YANCEY TAKES A CHANCE

I was a guy who struggled in school. I was petrified to even stand up and speak in classroom. The whole notion of the teacher saying, "Mr. Yancey. come up here and read the third chapter or these two pages." I would be petrified!

I was one of these kids who didn't have good study habits. When those tests came, I had this philosophy: I'm going to flunk this test. So rather than sit here and languish over it, I'd be the first one to turn in my paper so I that could mess up the thinking of all the smart kids. I was getting an F, so I might as well get it with style. But I didn't apply myself back then. I didn't see the linkage back then.

My background is musical. At an early age, I was a drummer in a band called Sun. In 1976 we came out with our first album with Capital Records and had numerous number one songs all across the market, all across the country. We had a great time for about five years. A band is like a business; it has the same structure. The band had great leaders and great creative people.

I ended up leaving the band and was working on my own deal to get my own recording career and producer's career. Along the way, I was burning up resources and record royalties. I thought, I'm not going to be able to sustain for very long if I don't create some kind of ongoing revenue stream outside of music. So I ended up doing some jingles.

Those jingles ended up attracting a number of clients who asked me to take over all of their advertising. I'd just do jingles for them, and they would ask if I could I do graphics and media buys, and could I write copy? I ended up developing my own advertising agency in Ohio. I've had struggles along the way; I've gone through cash flow problems, I've gone through tough times. I wondered, "How am I going to pay these salaries?" But those are operations issues. I overcame every one of them, and I've never missed a payroll.

Being in advertising, I really learned the power of messages. Before when we'd play music or write lyrics, there were songs and lyrics that I wrote that were very hollow. Once I got into advertising, I realized the power of the message and the words and how the same skills you use to shift people to go buy a car or go buy a mattress, or whatever. Those same things are being deployed in all the messages, whether it be your attitude about sexuality, women, or your job or career. I really learned the power of what you ingest through your mind is every bit as dangerous as what you ingest through your mouth, if you want to be healthy, emotionally as well as physically.

My agency grew to 40 employees and $20 million in annual sales. We handled all kinds of incredible accounts all over the Midwest. I did that for over 15 years. During that time, I won over 200 creative awards of excellence: I was Ohio's Black Businessman of the Year, and I was a finalist for *Ink Magazine's* Entrepreneur of the year.

CHANGING DIRECTIONS

Along the path of doing what you do, things emerge, and things open up to you. When I was 39 years old, I was bored with the advertising agency and I was actually ready for a change in my life. But because I owned a business, and because I had all these employees, I thought I should stay. I thought I should just ride this out.

Then one of my clients in Texas launched a positive TV network. On a visit there to go over some strategies, he said to me, "What would it take to get you to take over the global marketing for this TV network and do it full-time?"

> "The biggest risk is not taking any risk... In a world that changing really quickly, the only strategy that is guaranteed to fail is not taking risks."
>
> **Mark Zuckerberg**

This was a wealthy, wealthy individual. It really opened up an opportunity and a window I had never considered before. I actually put together a structured deal and he met my offer; he met what I needed to have to do this. So I sold my advertising agency to my employees and I moved to Dallas.

When I went to Dallas to take over the advertising and marketing for this TV network, I never even thought about the fact that I was actually going to work for an organization. I was an entrepreneur, soI saw it as, I'm going to this organization to lead this initiative, to lead this role. I saw myself as independent even in the structure of a corporation. What is significant about that was my mindset. So I went to work there, and I acted no differently how I owned my own company. And the guy I was working for, I felt like he was my partner.

I did that for two years. It was growing and doing great. Then the network decided to expand in some other areas and markets and ways that took it off of its core mission. I was fine with that, but I thought, "I've done my run here." I resigned from that position, and everyone was really great and wonderful to me.

That was the late 1990s, during the time of the big internet boom. It seemed like you could have socks.com and become a millionaire. It seemed like everyone was getting financed. Now all of a sudden, I was available to do new and exciting things. It was a new frontier.

At the TV network I made a lot of friends, and one of the guys was out of San Diego. He had put together an investor group that unbelievably wanted to bring on three marketing experts to come up with ideas for the internet. He called me and said, "Kym, I've got venture capital money, and I've told people about you and we're going to find three different experts in marketing that we want to get behind and finance their ideas and make you a part of it, and give you stock in it. It's going to be an idea incubator." For a marketing guy, you couldn't have said it any better.

LEARNING ALONG THE WAY

My wife and kids stayed in Dallas, and I would leave on Monday morning and fly to San Diego. I had a condominium on the beach in La Jolla, and then I'd come back Friday afternoon every week. My wife and my kids would come out some weekends and we'd have a great time.

My role was to come up with ideas that could be sold for the Internet. There were three of us. One guy focused on golf, another guy focused on real estate, and I decided to focus on building communities for African Americans, Hispanics, Asians, and women. I decided that the first thing I was going to do was to create a community for black professionals when it came to their career, dating, and networking.

I created the website www.ERT1.com that was an acronym for Each One, Reach One, Teach One. I designed the whole look for the website. Before it launched, several people wanted to buy it. They wanted to buy this concept that black professionals could go to this website and find out about careers, dating and networking. The interesting thing was, I had reached out to other people and organizations that already had expertise in those areas to help me build out the site.

At the time I went to Monster.com to do the career piece, I said, "This is what I'm doing, would you be interested?" They said they wanted to be a partner and put together the structure for professionals to find careers. Then I went to another company called MatchMaker.com, which happened to be in Dallas. I said, "I'd love to use your technology to create this dating portal for black professionals." They said they'd love to do that with me. There was no Facebook or LinkedIn at the time for anyone to do anything on the networking side, so I had to build that out myself.

MatchMaker was so smitten with the idea, they said, "Not only do we like what you are doing, but we'd like to buy the company, and we'd like you to come to work for us and lead a whole division around building out communities for black professionals, Hispanics, Asians and women." So within 5 months of creating the website, I had somebody who had already bought it.

The company that bought it was back in Dallas, so I moved right back to Dallas, and I became the VP of specialty markets for MatchMaker.com. But, before I could get anything finished, MatchMaker was sold to Lycos for millions of dollars. And it all ended—in a good way. I wasn't upset or unhappy about it. I cashed out, I got stock. But the website never launched. It got sold. Today Lycos doesn't even exist. Talk about how fast the market goes.

A NEW CONCEPT

But here's what happened. Here is what I learned. My wife has her master's degree in organizational development and is experienced in business. Once we moved to Texas, she didn't have a network, and we had our kids, so she didn't want a full-time job. So she was just doing consulting work. I said to her, "Sandra, you have a few consultant clients—big ones, too, like Coca Cola, and John Deere and different people like that—but there are all these other major corporations in Dallas. I'm sure if they knew you existed they would want to hire you. You have a unique problem.

"You have skills and talents that you can provide to these corporations who are looking for you, but they don't know your name, they don't know how to find you, and you don't know who to talk to in those corporations. If you've got that problem, I can only imagine that millions of other people have the same problem."

That led to the start of the eWomenNetwork, which is what we've been doing for 15 years now. It's a network that was all designed to help women connect, network, do business with each other, share resources with each other, and that turned into one of the, if not THE biggest women's business networks in North America. It is by far the most active and successful women's business network with 118 chapters across the United States and Canada; over 50,000 women are con-

> "The greatest discovery of all time is that a person can change his future by merely changing his attitude."
>
> **Oprah Winfrey**

nected through these chapters. We do almost 2,000 networking events every single year, including one of the largest international women's business conferences in North America, held in Dallas ever year, a 4-day business conference.

We put together a whole system and it just grows and grows and grows. It's helping more women become millionaires and successful, and live a life of happiness, and it's really created a network for these women all over the country to support each other.

GET PAST NEGATIVE THINKING

My biggest struggle in my personal life has been my own thinking. I have focused on how I've limited myself, or how I have not educated myself, or allowed myself to be compassionate, more understanding, or more kind. My biggest struggle earlier in my life was being more "me" focused than "other" focused. All of my challenges are rooted in my own thinking.

My biggest struggle in business is the same thing—it has always been myself. It's always been my own personal doubts or fears or not asking for help, or not doing the level of research that I needed to do and being in too big of a hurry. My single biggest struggle is my own thinking. It's how I look at things.

Out of all the business people I talk to, and I think for anybody, they may not say it this way but I think that we are our biggest cheerleader and distraction. I think it's our thinking.

So I have to constantly work at paying more attention and not beat myself down. Instead I try to be a little self compassionate with myself and say, "Listen, you've gone farther than you can ever imagine."

Today, I live in a $2 million home. I was in my pool the other day by myself, just floating and thinking. I said, "Dear God, thank you. I've done it. I am living in a house far beyond anything I thought I would ever live in. I have a fabulous family, I have a great wife, I'm doing work that's meaningful and has purpose and helps people, I'm not in pain. I'm floating around in this pool. I can't believe I've done this. And I want nothing more." What I want to do is, I want to serve. I realize that I want to serve and help more people.

Mark Cuban, said, "Most people don't do the work. Most people say they want to succeed, they want to be successful, they want to see their career or business grow. But they don't want to do the work—they really don't. It's talk and not the work to go with it." What I've learned from this, when I look at mindset, is even when you do the work, if you're doing the work, and you're working hard and putting your time into make something materialize for yourself, and you find that you're not getting the traction—that is the time to ask for help.

I was at a conference and a young man came up and asked me if I could consider being his mentor. I told him I was flattered, but my time was limited. I said, "But I've got something that's really outstanding for you. Have you ever heard of Stephen Covey's book *The 7 Habits of Highly Effective People?* It is one of my all-time favorite books. I've never met Stephen Covey, but he's been a great mentor to me. It was the words on those pages in that book that I studied." And not only his, but all kinds of books, but that's one of my favorites because it really nails it. You talk about somebody mentoring you, you couldn't get the content out of that.

The kid smiled. He went back to where he was sitting in the session, and he brought up his briefcase. He opened it and pulled out a copy of *The 7 Habits of Highly Effective People.* I told him, "That's what you need! That is an unbelievable mentor for you right here. And the mentor is in the book." He was taking proactive steps and got a book like this.

There are going to be people in your life you're around who are going to mentor you. Or there will be people you're going to see, and through their actions and behavior they offer mentorship, and you also meet and talk with them and get some feedback.

YOU HAVE TO ACT

We live in a time where if you struggle with money, you don't understand finances and credit, you can get on the Internet and you can look up all sorts of things: What's a Bull Market? What's a Bear Market? What's the DOW mean going up and down? How can I have good credit?

All kinds of content is available to you right through your computer, but you have to be willing to work and invest the time. You have to push yourself away from the television and from people who are negative or who aren't expanding your thinking.

Take a simple thing like diet. Look at our obesity rate in this country. Most people know what to do. Any adult man or woman knows what to do. You know that eating potato chips is not going to be good for your metabolism. It comes down to this—do you want to do it? Do you want to work hard at it? Do you want to do the work necessary? And if you don't want to do it, then be ok with the results that you're going to get instead of beating yourself up and saying, I've got to lose weight, I've gotta do this, or I've gotta do that.

Every step of the way there are decisions to be made. I've also learned to be a little more compassionate with myself, and to give myself a little bit of a break when I say, "Look, I am do-ing the best that I can." I can't let somebody's ending be my middle, or someone's middle be my beginning. We all have the capacity to get, do and be anything that we want to be if we are willing to invest in it.

WORKING WITH HIS WIFE

It's fabulous working with my wife on eWomenNetwork. We've been together 38 years. I wouldn't have thought we'd be that couple that would end up working together and owning a business together. I've watched my wife evolve and become this incredible businesswoman. I mean incredible. It's far beyond what she could have ever imagined for herself. And then the fun we get to have as a couple. Then how as a man, how I've had to evolve; I've had to learn a lot of lessons.

My biggest personal success is my relationship with my wife. We have struggled, too. We have gone through really dark times. She and I joke about how neither one of us wanted a divorce on the same week. What I have found is, she respects me and I respect her. I've learned the importance of her being her own woman, and giving her space to be her own woman. And she's always given me the space to be my own person.

She's never said anything unkind to take me down. When we were going through tough times, she never diminished how I felt as a man. She never put me down. I think it's critical for both. I think it's critical that a man never diminishes a woman, and a woman never diminishes a man.

You've got to lift each other up. We're fortunate that we have that kind of relationship. We're not Ozzy and Harriet. We've had our struggles. But I've gotta say, we rarely fight. Now, after 38 years we've learned a lot about each other.

I think especially for men, it's learning how to compromise, how to not be right. It's learning how to let go of thinking, "It's my way or the high way." The question you gotta ask yourself is, how is that working for you? One of the things that kills people—it affected me, it killed me at the beginning—is expectations. I'm not talking about not having expectations, I'm talking about having unreal expectations. I want to be treated this way, I want to be greeted this way.

You can be very, very disappointed with unrealistic expectations. Not only with your spouse, but with your kids, with your friends, with anything, with your job, your career. If you want to find something wrong with it, you can find it. Some people look for what's wrong like they're looking for the prize. It's there if you look for the dirt. I've learned to be first. To be first with a smile, first with the how you doing, first with the compliments.

KYM YANCEY'S FIVE SUCCESS & WEALTH TIPS

1. **Constantly invest in your own development by reading and attending events.** Keep stimulating your thoughts. If all you're doing is recycling the same info over and over again, you're not going to grow. You get to the point where

you start to recycle other people's thinking. Get out and meet new people. Go to conferences and go to different events. Because there you are going to meet new people and get new ideas. It's very important to get out and experience new things and new places.

I also tell people it's important to invest in experiences with your family and people. If you're making a choice between getting this new BBQ grill or going on a vacation—you're going to have a lot of fun with that grill, but I'm going to tell you something, when you're on your death bed, you won't remember that BBQ grill, but you're going to remember that experience you had on some vacation or something you guys did as a family, or something you did that's a memory. You will always remember those experiences far above the items.

You will remember the experience. That's something that will stay with you. It's books, it's building your network, it's getting out and meeting people, those are the things that matter; so be a veracious learner.

2. **Be grateful.** Wake up every day and think of three new things that you are grateful for. An attitude of gratitude is going to allow you to be more open and appreciative and enjoy. That's so critical.

3. **Your happiness is now.** You and I are in our "good old day" right now. Happiness is contagious, happiness is a

choice. Making the decision to be happy, and I'm going to spread happiness. I'm going to be around people that are happy. I'm going to be optimistic and have a positive attitude. People are attracted to people who are happy and have a smile on their face.

4. **Ask for help.** When you find yourself in trouble and can't figure it out, ask for help. That's going to come in a variety of forms. Some of that help is going to come from research that you do, asking friends or letting people know you are struggling in this area, or that area. But be willing to ask for help.

5. **Kindness.** You'll never be accused of being too kind. Be compassionate and kind to people. Then you can really cultivate relationships.

CHAPTER 7:
BEING TRULY FREE

Peggy Hightower

 *Peggy Hightower had tried life the conventional way—go to school, get a job, try to make a living. She was doing it, but she wasn't happy. Even as a registered nurse, it wasn't easy making ends meet, especially as a single mom.*

She dreamed of being financially free. She talked about her dream with friends, a dream they also shared, and so she jumped at the chance when presented with a business opportunity. But she was surprised when others didn't jump at it and still others were skeptical.

Now Peggy is a high earning network marketer who holds nothing back. She lives life to the fullest and is grateful that she took a chance, because now she is truly free. Read in Peggy's own words her journey to where she is today.

PEGGY HIGHTOWER'S LONG SUCCESSFUL LIFE

I think network marketing is really a blessing for America. Period. It allows you to have freedom. Commissions vs. salaries. I think all of those things are awesome. I was blessed to choose a network marketing company that the product is money.

So many people that live a long life—they could be 60, 70, or 80 years—but they have never been free. I'm very, very proud when people make a decision that they'll grow, and trust God, and become free.

And so if you're looking at going into business—you're going to have struggles, no matter what arena you're in. So why not go into an arena that will allow you to make money?

I got into the field from wanting knowledge about finances. I was not able to read the stock pages. I wasn't able to read my life insurance policy; I found out I had the wrong type of life insurance and wondered why a college graduate and a supervisor and a go-getter and a person who is calling themselves intelligent would make all of these financial errors.

I realized it was because of lack of knowledge. So I came looking for knowledge, not even thinking about building a business.

The biggest struggle I faced in business was rejection from those people who I thought would be on board with me, who I thought would have the same kind of zeal and desire that I had for freedom and knowledge and understanding. Prior to coming

There is no easy walk to freedom anywhere, and many of us will have to pass through the valley of the shadow of death again and again before we reach the mountaintop of our desires.

Nelson Mandela

into this business, we often talked at lunch hours and on breaks at work about how it would be great to be able to control how much money you made, to have some kind of freedom to live how you wanted to live, to drive what you wanted to drive. Ultimately we talked about those dreams every day.

But when the opportunity came to have those dreams come true, it was as if everybody ran into their respective corners saying, "Oh no but I don't want to do that." So that was a rejection that took me a minute to embrace. It's hard when the people around you tend to not want you around because you're talking about something they're not interested in. Before that, we tend to think that those people who are labeled family and friends are our connections to life.

I don't feel like I've accomplished anything. I know what I'm most excited about, and that's an opportunity to want to talk to me or call me. I can give them information about growing spiritual or economically. I count it a privilege to be able to tell people how important their spiritual growth is, no matter how much money they have, and them realizing that if you're growing spiritually you

> "In the end, it's not the years in your life that count. It's the life in your years."
>
> **Abraham Lincoln**

need to grow economically so that you'll be able to help and be significant. That's my greatest joy.

There are so many people I've been able to help in that arena that they're not necessarily in my business, or they've gone to other businesses, but because of my steadfastness and spirituality, they're growing in life and that's a plus. There are folks that have gone into other businesses; they fought for freedom.

FINANCIAL FREEDOM LATER IN LIFE

I have a couple of friends whose husbands have died or are dying. One has already moved out of their house, and another has their house up for sale. Not because they wanted to move out, but they're not financially able to stay.

With my husband making his transition to go home to glory recently, I'm just so blessed. Even with going through the transition of seeing him later and not having him now, I don't have to worry about finances. In fact, I'm thinking about where my second home will be.

I'm just so thankful that I did the long nights and sacrificing during that time. Now, I go in my office maybe a couple of hours a month.

To be in the top 1% of females in the USA, I'm so very thankful. I am also thankful that there are other people coming behind, that I would like to think I had something to do with it that are going for those high 6-figure incomes, and they'll hit it before I did.

Personal life and business life is kind of like heaven and earth. What's loosed in heaven is loosed on earth. What people don't realize is they loosed so much on earth, through their mouth. So someone will say, "I don't have no money today, I'm gonna lose my car, I'm gonna lose my house."

So the angels gotta go up in heaven and say, "They're expecting to lose their house!" Instead we should be saying, "All of my needs are met, according to you richness and glory." They're synonymous.

PEGGY HIGHTOWER'S FIVE SUCCESS & WEALTH TIPS

1. **Make a decision that you want to be wealthy.** Once you make a decision that you want to be wealthy, decide what that wealth is for you. Then when you figure out whatever business you will be in, decide that it won't just be you who is going to make you wealthy, but that you will have an opportunity to have a team.

Everybody who has gained some financial success in the USA, there's a team, even the superstar on the football team or the basketball team, but it's a team.

2. **Build a team of people who think like you.** The Bible says, I came to separate and divide mother from father, sister from brother, so if there's somebody around you who you've been calling friend or whatever, and they're not empowering you, maybe not listening to you, and embracing what you're doing, I would say you need to learn to cut yourself apart from those that are not on your side. A lot of people get caught up on that particular arena.

3. **You need a mentor.** Because you've not been in that position before, so you need someone who has been there and knows where to go.

4. **You mus be willing to change.** Sometimes change hurts. But you must be willing to take that pain. In order to change, you must be reading your spiritual devotions and reading about the mindset, because you've gotta change your mind set. In order to grow you've gotta have a renewing of your mind because now you're thinking wealth. Anybody can do poverty; poverty is the easiest thing in the world to do. But when you start talking about wealth, there's a lot more that you need to know.

5. **Become a student of your business.** You don't have to do all of it, but you have to know all of the details of your business.

CHAPTER 8:
BELIEVE IT'S POSSIBLE

Ruben West

 *Ruben West was serving our country when the introduction of an opportunity to be an entrepreneur came in an unlikely way. But isn't that how the best opportunities come? They come without us expecting or being quite ready. So with faith we have to jump in and trust that it's right.*

Jumping in is the test. Will we jump? Will we believe that we can do it? Will we believe it's possible?

Ruben believed, even though those around him didn't. When you have a new idea, a new concept, it's not comfortable for everyone. They just don't understand the vision. But be like

Ruben and don't let it back you down. Eventually, you'll show them the way and even inspire others to do the same.

Read in Ruben's own words how he believed it was possible.

RUBEN WEST'S INNER WAR

Life is a roller coaster. There are good times and there are bad times. If we could predict when they were, then that would be easy because we know when all the good times were. And then we would know when all the bad times were. And so we could govern ourselves to work on all the good times, and then govern ourselves to work on all the bad times.

But there is no set way. If your family is doing good, then the business could be doing bad. Sometimes the business is doing good, and your personal life is going bad. Then sometimes they're both doing good, and then sometimes they're both doing bad.

So here's what you learn—that you have to take the good with the bad. That's all called life. It's a balancing act. It's not IF you will have problems. It's WHEN.

> "Faith is taking the first step even when you don't see the whole staircase."
>
> **Martin Luther King, Jr.**

There are three types of problems in life: the ones you've been through, the ones you're going through right now, and the ones that are waiting on you. And so if you're not in a difficult time right now, wait a couple of weeks.

When I was in the Gulf War, I had the chance to meet a surgeon who said, "Ruben, I want to teach you how to assist. Because in war there is no 9-5. I want to teach you how to assist." I said ok. Fortunately, the war didn't last that long. The ground war only lasted 72 hours, but keep in mind that we had more patients than that because there was a lot of other stuff still going on.

I am thankful for that opportunity. I got a glimpse into what I could be. Albert Einstein said, "Imagination is a preview of what's to come." When I had that experience, I imagined I could go back home and be a surgical assistant. Only, that position didn't exist in the state of Kansas. You could be a PA, a nurse practitioner, or another doctor, but there were no surgical assistants. And so that's what got me thinking about starting the profession and then being one. I caught a glimpse into that possibility.

I believe that's the way it shows up for everyone. That we get a glimpse of what we could be, and then we have to put in the work to make it a reality. Now, at the same time we're putting in that work, we're changing who we are to become the person who could be in that space, because who we are right now can't occupy that space.

That's why when you give the people that win the lottery the winnings, a lot of them file bankruptcy within five-seven years—because they didn't have a wealth mindset. They weren't they type of person who could handle that kind of money, and you just gave it to them. It's different when you have to build wealth over the years, than when it's just handed to you.

It's like that with many things in life. If somebody had just handed me a surgical assistant company, it would have failed. But since I had to grow it and build it, I had to learn how to keep it going.

FRIENDLY FIRE

The biggest struggle in business and in your personal life is belief. To me, that's what it comes down to on a lot of fronts. The belief that I could do it. Because you have to look at all the people who will tell you that you can't do it.

In the military, we were at war. And one of the biggest mishaps of war is called friendly fire. It's when you accidently get your own men with ammunition or bombs. Even though they're your people, it still does damage. If you're going to go after your dream, if you're going to start your business, you've got to be aware of the concept of friendly fire. A lot of times, the people you love and care about are telling you that you can't do it.

"What are you thinking? How is that going to work?"

You have to believe in yourself, if spite of what other people are saying. We were instructed to walk by faith, not by sight. We were instructed to judge not according to appearances. In spite of what they're saying and what it looks like, you have to say, "I could do this anyway."

The hardest thing for me at times was to believe because sometimes I was thinking, this isn't lining up. What I should see isn't there, and I don't know if I'm going to make it. But you have to have the ability to just keep going through those periods of time where you're doubting yourself.

For me, the hardest thing was the belief that eventually it would come to pass if I just stayed the course. In your personal life when you're doing those things, if you don't have the people by your side who believe in you, it causes problems. Because you're always juggling.

People are supportive of you if they feel like what you are doing is going to lead to a benefit of them. If you're going to medical school, they get it. It's ok to sacrifice now because when you become a doctor, that will change everything for all of us. They get that because a doctor is a very regimented pathway, it's been done over and over again, it's replicateable and duplicateable and people have done it.

However, when you're setting out to be an entrepreneur—and what you're setting out after hasn't been done before—then you don't get that same support. And so the struggle is keeping them engaged and enrolled in the possibility that this is going to happen not only for me, but for us. It's going to change all of our lives.

My biggest accomplishment is making my vision become a reality. And it is not a singular statement. When I said I was going to have a martial arts school, many people didn't believe that. After a period of time and putting in the work, it came to pass. And now I've had it for over 17 years.

When I said I was going to have a surgical assistant business, and when I said I was going to BE a surgical assistant, people didn't believe me. I set out to be one so that surgeons would be able to call me and say, "Ruben come in and help me," and I'd just be able to walk in and help them at any hospital. Well, I've done that, too! Don't let what other people say keep you from what you want most.

INSPIRING OTHERS TO CHANGE

My biggest accomplishment is to inspire others. I feel great when people say to me, "Ruben, I had an idea and I didn't know if I could do it. But I saw your Martial Arts school, or I saw the things you've done, and it encouraged me to go after what I want." When you can inspire someone else to follow in your footsteps because you stepped out in faith, you believed in the vision that you were given, to me that's the ultimate accomplishment because of the ripple effect. You're making a difference in the world. You're changing the world.

I want this to be my accomplishment for my children—to believe that whatever they want, they can achieve. That it doesn't already have to have been done before—it could or it couldn't, it doesn't matter. They don't have to be entrepreneurs like me, it doesn't make a difference. What they have to be is what they choose to be. I want them to believe that they can do it. That's my accomplishment. But I won't know it until I'm gone; they'll meet me and tell me in heaven, "Dad, I went and did it."

> "Think of yourself where you eventually want to be in pursuit of your own successes. What will you say to the person you are right now?"
>
> **Ruben West**
> *Destination Mastery*

Currently I do motivational, inspirational, and transformational speaking. I also do coaching and training to give people the tools to do the work. People like the motivation, and they like the inspiration, but what I realize is that you have to give them the tools so they can put in the *perspiration*. Because that's what's going to make the difference—the difference is in the action that you take. I want to get them to take action and give them the tools to do it.

The most difficult thing for me to do was to believe that I could do it. But now that I've done it, I can use my skills and talents and thinking to help other people believe that they can do it. And now I realize I have the ability to train people to be able to speak so that when they speak to people, it changes their belief system and what's possible for their lives.

RUBEN WEST'S FIVE SUCCESS & WEALTH TIPS

1. **Do what makes your heart sing.** I believe the only way you can give your all to something, is that if whatever that something is brings it out of you. If you're doing something that's just a job, it's never going to bring that out of you. You're always going to get frustrated. You're always going to get tired. You're always going to get irritated. A lot of people put themselves in that situation and they go through it again and again, and they die in that situation.

   I believe most people are dying, not because of what they're eating but because of what's eating them. They know that what they've been doing is not what they've been called to do. And so the first thing they have to do is this: they have to make sure that they can align themselves with their calling. Now that doesn't mean that you can't have a job, but you can do things in addition. For example, if you want to volunteer, or work doing an after school program, or work with the youth or work with the elderly, or start a side business. No matter what it is, do it! Not everybody is cut out to be an entrepreneur, so you can look at other avenues.

   There are things that we are *paid* to do and things we are *made* to do. Everybody is cut out for something, whatever it is that they know that they're made to do, they have to find a way to be involved in that. Because that doesn't take their life, that gives them life. Be involved in something that you're passionate about.

2. **Have a dream that's big enough for other people's skills and talents.** I saw a guy pushing a car. He was stopped at a stop light and his car had run out of gas. The door was open and he was trying to push it forward. I knew it wasn't going to work. You can't push the car and try to steer it, but he was still trying. After a while I thought, I will go help him.

I pulled my car over and I jumped behind his. Pretty soon, it was me and him, and a number of people helping to push. Then after a while the car was going so fast he had to jump in the car and shut the door and just guide it to the gas station.

The point is, when we saw him working, we were willing to work. But if he had been sitting in the car saying, "Hey, come push my car!" We would not want to help.

Whenever you're going after something, make it big enough for other people's skills and talents. Even if you're not able to do it by yourself, the fact that you're going after it is and invitation for other people to help you and for the universe to collaborate in your favor.

3. **Accept that life is a roller coaster.** You will not have all good days, and you will not have all bad days. There are going to be ups and downs. And they're going to hit you. No one is exempt! Even if you're doing good. Some people think that if they're doing something to help other people, or that's positive or beneficial to society, that

they're not going to get hit. Well, it's not that type of party. They'll steal your car, too. So just because you're investing in something that's positive, it doesn't mean that you're going to get out of the waves of life. We have to expect it.

4. **Don't stop.** A lot of times, we get to the point where we don't know if we're going to make it. So we start questioning if we can make it. But don't ask that! The question is not, are you not going to make it? The question is, can you take the next step? If we don't focus on making it way over there, then it doesn't seem so daunting.

All you focus on is, how do I take this next step? Because a 26-mile marathon is just based on a number of steps. And it has to start with the first one and it has to end with the last one. But they're all individual steps. So when you're overwhelmed, don't look at the big picture—bring it down to the small picture. Remember why you set out to do it, the difference you were going to make, and focus on taking that next step.

5. **Inspire other people to take steps in their passion, because no one does it alone.** Just like I talked about with pushing the car, when you are taking the steps, you encourage other people to take steps. Then your life becomes an inspiration. Then people will just look at you and want to be around you because they're drawn to your accomplishment and they're drawn to your determination and they're drawn to your internal leadership.

So your job is to not only make it, but to help other people make it. Whenever you get to the point where you can lend a hand to help somebody else take the next step, that's what you have to do. Once you get to the point where you can help someone take that next step, your job is to help them take it. Because in doing so, you go up higher. You are surrounding yourself with people who are winners and who have learned to win.

CHAPTER 9:
NO BAD DAYS

Steve McCaffery

Steve McCaffery knows success and he knows failure. But he professes that he never has bad days. Of course, he does have challenges, but he doesn't focus on those. He hits them head on and gets past them.

Ultimately, we live and we learn. And if we are positive and move forward, then success will come. Failure can be a good teacher, especially if we approach it with a good attitude.

Steve has a good attitude no matter what. In his soul, what he wants is to help people. And that will definitely equate to no bad days. Read in his own words how he became an unlikely entrepreneur.

STEVE MCCAFFERY'S ACCIDENTAL ENTREPRENEURSHIP

I got started in this field by accident. I was first exposed to public adjusting in 1985. My parents were referred to a public adjuster when they had inspections of damage at their house. They were told by the public adjuster that normally the damage they had would have been covered, except they had a policy that was a standard fire policy. He explained to them that they should go out and get a homeowner's policy and specifically to ask the agent for an HO3.

They did, and they ended up getting better coverage. So instead of having a standard fire policy, they had an HO3 all-risk policy; they had more coverage on their contents, more coverage on the building, and more coverage and lower liability, and their premiums were less.

That was a little bit of a wakeup call. I said, "Why would they have bought that other policy?" They bought that other policy like most Americans do. When they are buying their house, they turn to their real estate agent. The real estate agent says, buy this or buy that. So they were sold a standard fire policy, which is a high risk policy. Is there any reason you would need a high risk policy?

Insurance companies have to treat areas based on risk for everyone, and everyone's in a pool. Companies used to do illegal red-lining. Managers used to tell their agents, "You could sell policies and all this state except for these areas." State regulators found this to be discriminatory.

I always explain to people, "You better get your policy checked out." With insurance, you have to find out about a policy before you ever have a loss; because once you have the loss, you're locked into the current policy and then you're stuck. That was my first exposure developing a policy review that we still use today.

One of the things as a business owner is that I don't have "bad" days. In business and in life, I have always found that it doesn't really matter what comes, you just have to be positive. You have to be focused, and you have to maintain a great attitude. I forget about the bad things. It's a learned experience to forget about the bad things. As a business owner and being successful, you really need to focus on the good things and put the blinders on like a horse race. Look at the objective.

DECIDING TO CHANGE YOUR LIFE

You have to look at your past and think, when did I make a decision to make a difference in my life? As a kid, I grew up poor. It was a blue collar neighborhood; people went to work but they didn't make high wages. There was a period of time that my mother was on welfare because she didn't have a job, and she raised us without a father.

It was a struggle. We always had presents at Christmas, we always had a birthday cake on our birthdays, but I always remember as a kid that I felt like that we were poorer than the other poor people in our neighborhood.

> "My mission in life is not merely to survive, but to thrive; and to do so with some passion, some compassion, some humor, and some style."
>
> **Maya Angelou**

I always thought, what am I going to do? As a kid of 10 years old, I wanted to become successful. I didn't know how to define that. But I remembered thinking that I wanted to find a way to be more successful in life.

My mother got remarried and I had a step-father. They were able to get me into my first year of Catholic high school and then from that point forward, I was able to work jobs to pay for the rest of my high school, because I wanted to study and get that Catholic education. I felt like it was a good education.

I wasn't the brightest bulb in the class. I struggled to get into Penn State. I by-passed the normal requirements; based on just a regular application, I wasn't going to be accepted. But as soon as you start taking some courses and passing them, then they'll accept you as a full time student. So I got by that hurdle.

I switched majors several times and took more time to go through college than normal—6 ½ years. During those years, I was in a motorcycle accident, which put me in the hospital for six weeks. A friend brought me a book by Dr. Wayne W. Dyer called *Your Erroneous Zones*. I read the book cover to cover. It was the first part of training my thinking.

In reading, I learned that you have to focus on what you can change and not focus on what you can't change. The book really focused on how we allow situations to influence the way we feel, because those situations are controlling us. And he pointed out how if you learn to see the situation and what's out of your control, and realize it's out of your control and not allow that to affect you, then you're going to be able to be more focused and positive on a situation. That started my thinking process.

I worked as a public adjustor part-time while I was still a student. It was always a great source of income. But I'd seen another opportunity for selling life insurance for A.L. Williams, now known as Primerica. I made a premature decision to quit my regular job to commission only at A.L. Williams. I loved the training, but it wasn't the easiest thing in the world for me to sell life insurance. I did all the wrong things. I spent more money than I made. I charged up credit cards to pay for gas and to entertain people with meals and entertainment and go to functions. I found myself accumulating so much debt and having a lack of income, I got to a breaking point and walked away after a year and a half. It was my first real exposure to network marketing and multi-level marketing. I love the concept. I loved A.L. Williams so even though it didn't work out for me, I didn't have any regrets.

So I got a job as a general contractor for a doctor making $15 an hour just to start getting some income. That was the start of the change. I thought, I've got to go back and start rebuilding myself. I was still writing some claims on the side, and one of the adjusters at the previous company was going to open up his own company. He opened Remmy Adjustment and wanted me to work for him.

I started working for him and we worked well together. That quickly turned from part-time to full-time, and that's where I started learning to do adjustments myself and build a team. To my boss, I introduced the concept (that we have today in my current company) to expand his company with bringing in and training people as public adjusters.

GOING OUT ON HIS OWN

I eventually left and took the opportunity to start Metro Public Adjustment in 1993 with a good core of people I trained and recruited from the previous company. It is a network marketing concept. It's an independent business owner building a business within a business. It's the franchise models. I've studied franchising and I love the franchise set up.

A lot of people think that businesses fail because they don't have enough money, but the number one reason businesses fail is because they don't know what they're doing. They don't have a system and a plan in place to make money. Obviously, if you have unlimited money you're going to continue to run your company. But if you're not making money you're not going to sustain yourself.

The reason you're not making money is you don't know what you're doing. You don't have the right managing staff in place, you don't have the right processes in place, so the concept of having a company that knows what they're doing and being an independent business owner internally within that company really excites me. It excited me back in 1993, it excites me today, and it's a big part of why I love this business.

I surround myself with entrepreneurs. Entrepreneurs have a different mindset. I love entrepreneurship. I love entrepreneurs because they have a desire to be better. They have a desire to be successful. They have a desire to be in their own business. That's different than someone just showing up and punching the clock and at the end of the day it's all off their minds. An entrepreneur lives and breathes their business.

They don't necessarily work 24/7, but if there's an opportunity they find, they're going to grab it; if they have the opportunity to talk or develop a new idea, they're going to discuss it. It doesn't matter what time it is, they're always on the clock. A friend of mine said, if you love what you're doing, you'll never work another day in your life. I love what I do. I still work.

There's not a day that goes by where there isn't some kind of challenge. But in 2007 we underwent huge challenges. We had some people who were officers of the company. They were sent to create a business deal for the company and then took that business deal for themselves. On top of that, they created a distraction for the company, so we lost our focus. The company sustained a $150,000 loss that year.

One of the turning points for Metro was in 2008 when I was approached by Vistage. (It used to be called The Executive Committee (TEC) started in the 1970s.) It was an organization that opened up the door for small to medium sized businesses to have professionals, almost like your own board, who you could turn to. Because sometimes when you're a small business, you're an island. Maybe no one agrees with you and you don't have a staff of people to turn to.

Vistage is worldwide. There are 400 member companies in the Philadelphia area, and our group has 16 people. We meet once a month. It's a group that talks about how we can run our businesses better. I get to meet once a month with the chair of the group, who's got a lot of experience and has run businesses that are worth several hundred million dollars. We get to talk on a one to one basis. We talk about the direction of our company and bounce ideas and strategies off of him both for the financial aspects and for the marketing aspects of the company.

Truly there's a number of different factors that are important in business. But if I had to come up with the most important to me, it's your mindset. You have a choice in life every single day to decide on to go in a positive direction or a negative direction. So you train yourself, and anyone can train themselves, to push aside the negative part of the day and focus on the positive.

NOT BACKING DOWN

The biggest challenge that I faced in Metro is that we were looking to be regulated out of business. We help people at all levels, and a number of organizations wanted to change that and make it difficult for us to represent everyone and only represent people with larger losses. That's when a national act was being developed for capping what public adjusters can charge in the business, which would prohibit us financially from being able to represent everyone.

That process was very scary. As a business owner I said, "We know that they're trying to do this, I don't know what we're going to do to stop it, I just know that we're going to stop it." I took the attitude that there was a solution out there, we just had to find it. We started organizing our attorneys and our managing staff. We had meetings to brainstorm what could we do to defeat this. Over a period of time we developed industry support, and other company sup-

"My advice would be to follow your dream. Most of my life, I was in second place before I came in first place. I hope that inspired people to never give up."

Jackie Evancho

port, and regulatory support. At the end of the process, the regulators agreed that homeowners should have the opportunity to have representation and we weren't capped in our fees. It worked.

It took place 2004-2005 and has paid dividends because it's been a model now, a good model for multiple states to adopt. Had we not defeated it at the time, and had they made the changes, these same states would have adopted that model and it would have been very problematic for our company.

In Metro Public Adjustment, the biggest accomplishment is as we break through each glass ceiling. Our first glass ceiling was that we were stocking around $5-6 million in revenue. And then we broke through the next glass ceiling at $10-12 million in revenue. And we're going to continue to break through those glass ceilings.

My CEO responsibility to the company is to continue to grow and expand, because if you're offering a business opportunity to someone, you have to have a commitment to those people that are signing on the dotted line. It's only a great opportunity if the company continues to expand.

We may have some struggles, but there's a 100% commitment that this company will continue to grow and innovate itself to be the leader in our business. Information changes, the technology changes, and we're changing with it. We've got a lot of commitment into technology, we have a commitment to growth, commitment into management and diversity as far as what can we do differently and what can we do to add on to what we're doing now.

SET YOUR PRIORITIES

Having five children is my biggest success in my personal life. I consider myself very blessed. Just watching my children grow and seeing their personalities and seeing that they're good people is wonderful. I believe that no business or personal life is successful unless you have priorities in life. For me that's God, family, and business. I take that very seriously. I start my day with prayer, and I turn to Jesus when I have a problem. I turn to him just to thank him every day. Most of it is praying for other people, and a lot of it is thanking God for the things that I have and for the life that I have. I also try to instill that in my children. We go to church every Sunday, we say grace at our dinner meal, and treating people properly is a big accomplishment in our family.

I'm no saint; I haven't done everything perfectly in my life, but I truly believe in treating everyone properly. A friend told me that you can't discipline your kids for everything; you have to pick and choose which ones are less important. There's one line that my children cannot cross, and that is respect. If they are disrespectful, they will be disciplined instantaneously. They all realize that so they never cross that line. They see a look that I give them and they know.

I've been very fortunate to have been married to my wife, who is very supportive of my business. I'm able to run my business and have a family life and personal life that is very happy. I've seen other business leaders when their family life is falling apart and their business really struggles.

Another key factor in business that has been important to me is self development and education. I've always read self books, gone to seminars for our business and seminars for personal development.

You need to surround yourself with key people. No one leader has all the answers. You may have a great idea; there's always someone better than you that can be on your team. First of all, recognize that you're not the smartest person in the room. I don't care what company you're running, or what idea you had, you're not the smartest person in the room.

In fact, there's one thing I learned early on in life, and that's if you've ever heard the term "arrogance," and if you understood the term arrogance to that level, an arrogant person thinks they're the smartest person and that there isn't a better idea. So make sure you're not arrogant; that's very important in business. If you're arrogant it's your downfall. Then, surround yourself with key people who are diversified in their thinking. Having a management team is very important to the success and growth of a company.

From the very beginning if someone is not sure and they want to start a business, and they want to get some insight into whether they should start a business, you could study all types of businesses. But there's a driving force. And the driving force is they have a vision and they take that vision and they say, this is what I'm going to do and then they make a decision. Everything else falls into place from there.

FINDING YOUR VISION

To start a business, first you have to have a vision of where you're going and what you're doing. If you want to open up a business and you have an idea, great, but if you want to be successful you have to see yourself in that vision. By far, one of the most important factors to being successful in business is to have a vision that you can be successful and you can go someplace. And second, you have to decide, because a vision without a decision is a dream.

It's like when you buy a lottery ticket. There's a value to buying lottery tickets; I still buy them from time to time, especially when the lottery's big because the $2 you spend is worth it. Anymore than $2 probably isn't worth it, but because you get to dream... wow if I suddenly had this instant amount of money what would I do?

Take that same thought process and say, my lottery ticket is actually my business. So if I won the lottery, how would my life be? That's really what you want it to be. Take that thought process and decide. You can start to set the landscape for what you want your life to be based on the fact of this $2 lottery ticket. It gives you a vision. And then you make the decision to achieve that; you think, I'm going to go after that.

Whatever your dream and vision is, it can adjust itself. It's going to change. Circumstances are going to change in life, and maybe you're not going to go as far as you thought, or things are going to go much greater. You may diversify your plan, vision, and goal a little bit, but for the most part you're going to be headed in the right direction. All the elements to get there are going to remain the same. But don't feel like if you didn't hit a certain milestone or a certain time period, that you're a total failure; you just had to readjust it.

The only way to fail is to quit. It's just to give up on the fact that you can succeed. There's story after story of success, where people kept trying and trying and eventually they became successful. In our company, when I hear of being people so close to being successful, and then they quit. I think, "No!"

Businesses need to have a momentum. Let's say you're a bakery, and you have a great cake product. People say, "Oh that was great, you've got to try Stock's Bakery." They tell their friends and all of a sudden that momentum starts to gain. People start to come there from referrals and then they have a good experience from the cakes and they come back for more. But what if a customer shows up one day and the doors are closed?

And you come back and the doors are closed? That's the same thing as quitting your business. Now you've lost all that goodwill and all that marketing and the doors are now closed.

Now you hope people will keep restarting. It's one thing to restart a new idea, it's another thing to quit and restart. Because you can maintain momentum by shifting your ideas and diversifying. But when you quit and stop, you lose your momentum. And literally you're starting over again. So that's a very important lesson to stick it out and not quit.

You don't have all the answers, but when you do self development and listen to key people who have had other experiences, you get the answers from that. When you have a problem or an idea, talk to someone about it. All of a sudden there's an idea born of two people talking; it's almost like a third person. This is known as the mastermind principle.

In business there will always be the people who are naysayers, and it's important to steer yourself away from that; watch who you take advice from because advice can come from the wrong person especially if they've never been in business. Also, some people are envious or jealous. They almost despise your success. When they see others fail, they get a sense of satisfaction because they've never had the opportunity to start a business and they say, "Well if I would have started a business it would have failed like your business."

In business you're going to have challenges. That mastermind person could be your parents, it could be your siblings, it could be a friend, it could be somebody in your company; so surrounding yourself with key people doesn't necessarily have to mean paid people or those on your management team. If you have an idea or a problem or a challenge, talk to somebody who is willing to provide you with solutions.

STEVE MACCAFFERY'S FIVE SUCCESS & WEALTH TIPS

1. Attitude equals attitude, so your mindset is very important.

2. Keep your priorities in order.

3. Develop your vision and goals and plans.

4. Stay positive.

5. Surround yourself with a good team and self development.

CHAPTER 10:
SHARE YOUR TALENT

Trevor Otts

Trevor Otts knows business. Not just how to make money, but how to give back. In essence, he looks at business as sharing your talent and helping others. Who wouldn't want to start their own business doing that?

No matter your talent, there are multiple opportunities out there waiting for you. Once you find out what they are, do them and then work smart. Be the CEO only, don't do everything. Build a team. Develop systems that sustain themselves. When challenges come, don't you dare give up.

Read in Trevor's own words about how he not only was able to earn a living through his talents, but how he was able to pass on his knowledge to the next generation of entrepreneurs.

TREVOR OTTS BELIEVES IN SERVING OTHERS

I'm in the field of helping people through my gifts and talent. My gifts and talent have really gone through an evolution. I've been in business most of my natural life. I sold my first product or service at the age of maybe 5 years old—it was a lemonade stand. Then I was bagging groceries. I was always looking for a way to sell a product or sell a service. In many ways the ability to be in business has been due to knowing how to package your talent or gift.

I sold cars, I owned a children's photography company, I owned a real estate company. Now I own full-service sales, marketing and automation firm. And you may say, how could you do all of that? The one thing I was able to do was I was always really good at marketing. And I was always good at positioning different products and services in such a way that caused people to take action. Specifically that action was buying.

One thing I will say about anybody who has a gift or has a talent is, don't get boxed in. You're not one gift, you're not one talent. There are things that you're good at and that show up in different ways in your field. I believe your gifts and your talents are meant to provide for you and meant to serve others. So when you serve others through your gifts, it will provide for you.

Conversely, if you try to serve *yourself* through your gifts, typically you will not make any money. A self-serving person never prospers. Is that the case in all scenarios? Probably not. But typically when you find someone who is self-serving, their circle is so closed, and they never welcome in the resources that they really need to become a prosperous, wealthy person.

If you're out there not generating enough wealth and enough revenue, my question would be, are you serving people through your gifts and talents? Just like gravity is a force, what goes up must go down. Think of service as a force. When you serve others, it will provide for you. Period. Once you accept that, once you believe that, it will affect your business outcome, revenue outcome, and wealth outcome.

Don't just do it, believe it.

Words affect beliefs, and beliefs affect outcome. I want to make sure I empower you with the right wealth-generating words. So that it affects your wealth-generating outcome and belief. So it also affects your wealth-generating outcome and your revenue outcome. Words affect beliefs and beliefs affect outcome. Change your beliefs and change your words, and you'll change your outcome.

CHIEF 'EVERYTHING' OFFICER

Disorganization is a struggle that a lot of entrepreneurs have—they do the marketing, they do the branding, they do the sales they do the labor, they do the accounting. They do everything. They are the CEO, which really becomes the Chief 'Everything' Officer. Because of that, they put themselves into a position where they're not doing anything particularly well in their business.

The first thing you want to do in business is create a hierarchy of your priorities and how you're going to get them done. Next, understand how people work in your organization. Here is a quick snapshot of that. Employees manage the tasks within a company. Supervisors manage the employees within a company. The CEO manages the processes and the procedures and the systems within the company.

What normally starts happening is you get CEOs who are performing more like supervisors or like employees. So then what happens is that many people in business never really get beyond the area of management, or they're supervising the other employees in the company. While they are supervising, they're not put-

> "We ourselves feel that what we are doing is just a drop in the ocean. But the ocean would be less because of that missing drop."
>
> **Mother Teresa**

ting in place systems. They're managing on the fly. They are managing by personality and charisma. They are managing in the moment. It's what I call reactionary processing, where the processes that they are producing are really just a reaction to a problem that came up.

They are always reacting to things. Because of that, it appears that they are getting results and are a success; but actually every time you are reacting to a situation vs. having put a plan in place, it is causing you to not put systems in place. That is not using your time wisely and being productive. The true CEO is always thinking about systems and process. When you have a system and process in place, it creates sustainable results.

When you don't have a system or process in place, you may have some success, but you will not be able to create the success that you will be able to sustain. One of the things we need to focus on as entrepreneurs is we must focus more on systems. Dare I say it, there is a level above the CEO, and that's the virtual CEO. That's the person managing the processes and the systems within your company automatically and virtually.

The CEO who needs to be hands on, needs to be right there in the shop—those days are gone. If you don't change you're going to die as a business owner; just go ahead and put up the sign that says, "Out of Business."

GOING FORWARD IN THE FACE OF DEFEAT

As an entrepreneur, you'll have times where money comes in and times where it doesn't come in. You rob Paul to pay Peter. You make that choice between choosing to pay the mortgage or choosing to pay the landlord at your business. I was running a 7 figure operation, and everything that you can imagine bad had happened.

I remember one night when I was working late. By the time I got home, they had already stolen all my stuff—my suits, my TV, my bags. I was left with about two bags of clothes. I was faced with a choice at that moment. What do I do? As far as I knew, I only had one way—forward. I needed to go back to work. I say this for all entrepreneurs out there. The way that an entrepreneur answers challenges is to really sell their way out of it.

It's easy to talk about getting up when you feel good. But it's hard to get up when you have a bankruptcy notice, or you got that pink slip on the apartment door. I remember my BMW got repossessed so many times, I knew the repossession guy. He would just knock on my door. He would knock on my door and say, "Hey Mr. Otts, you want to make sure everything's in tact, and get your stuff out real quick and give me the keys?"

So what did I do? I went back to work to sell my way out of it. That's the good news about being an entrepreneur—any moment in time you can create cash out of the air. As an entrepreneur, you have this innate power. The only other place in the entire world that has this power is the US Mint. The other person, they have to ask for overtime. They have to beg somebody, they have to borrow. They have to make promises they can't keep.

No matter how talented you are, no matter what you have going for you or going against you, no matter what pedigree you come with or certifications you come with, you cannot beat persistence. You gotta get up.

At the end of the day, you can't quit. You can't give up. If you're thinking that the right pedigree is going to never experience failure, you're wrong. You're absolutely wrong. You're going to learn more through failure then your successes. Entrepreneurship gives you some skin.

It's not like a job; with a job you can go get another one. If you lose it, you go get yourself some unemployment insurance. If you're an entrepreneur, there's no unemployment insurance for you. Knowing that it depends on you, it is all on you, while it does add suppression, it builds strong shoulders. And as an entrepreneur, you do shoulder a lot of responsibilities for the dreams and the hopes of people who serve with you. You shoulder the responsibility of delivering a quality product to those people who decide to work with your company.

TEACHING THE NEXT GENERATION OF ENTREPRENEURS

After we had been in business for a while, we became aware that it wasn't just generating money and revenue for ourselves, but it was really about creating legacies for those who had children we served in the community. One of our greatest accomplishments is we moved from becoming an entrepreneur to becoming an *impact*. Then we realized we could make a difference and a dollar at the same time.

So we created a program where every summer we were bringing in about 100 youth who we taught how to be entrepreneurs. We created this internship. Then the parents could come in and wondered when they would work. We told them, they start when we start. They end when we end. That's the life of an entrepreneur. Do you want your child to be an entrepreneur? Yes. Do you want them to be able to impact the lives of others? Yes. They start when we start and they finish when we finish.

Some of the children had some problems. Some used drugs, some smoked weed, some might have been playing too many video games. We would tell the parents, don't stop whatever bad habit they have. If they can hang with us and still keep their bad habit, they deserve it. What the parents came to realize was that their commitment to being an entrepreneur outweighs their commitment to their bad habit, and their child will give up their bad habits.

We never had to say, you have to stop doing this. Sometimes as parent we say the word stop. The problem is, stopping doesn't get anything done. Most parents need to have a replacement strategy. So what we did for children was we replaced some of the things that were disrupting their lives and we had a replacement strategy; we replaced them with things that allowed them to operate in creativity. So one of our greatest accomplishments is creating thousands of youth entrepreneurs throughout the world. We're really proud of that.

What's also interesting is we also saw a dramatic rise in their grades. If you can succeed as an entrepreneur, you can succeed at anything anywhere. You could drop me in the Mojave Desert, and I will figure out how to make a product and sell something. If it's selling product or selling fans, I put a marketing campaign to it. So my point is, the entrepreneur, once you hone their skill set, understand they can survive anywhere. It's sorta like dropping a Navy Seal; entrepreneurs are like Navy Seals.

I love that we are sowing into the lives of youth and business owners. One of the things I love about what we do is that we help the entrepreneur or that business owner who didn't have a shot—we believed in them. And I believe it's not just one accomplishment, it's an accomplishment we meet every day.

KEEPING DREAMS ALIVE

We understand that when someone brings their business, product, service or idea to us, they are depositing it in our trust. It's sort of like going to the bank. You expect that bank to keep your money safe and secure. And then in addition to that they give you a profit on the money you deposit.

So people bring you their ideas, business, product, service, or dream. What they are really doing is depositing it into your infrastructure. They want you to keep that dream safe and secure for them. To really make that dream and that inspiration profitable for them.

There will be times when they give up; but because they deposited their dream into your infrastructure, even when they give up, you hold the dream alive. Even when you stop believing, your infrastructure takes over and you believe for them. So one of our greatest accomplishments, or one that we personally accomplish every day, is the fact that we keep people's dreams alive. That we keep people's dreams moving forward, and we help people take their idea and make it profitable. Then I would say that we are a dream deposit institution, a dream incubator.

ENTREPRENEURSHIP IS A LIFESTYLE

Your business life and your personal life—sometimes they run parallel to each other. If you talk to any entrepreneur, there's almost no separation between their personal life and business life. They run very close to the same. A bad day in your business is a bad day in your personal life. You hear all sorts of stories, the guy who went bankrupt and got divorced. It seems like it all happens at the same time.

Business is holistic. You have to have a holistic approach to business. It's not separate. It's not work and home; it's this is my life. The big takeaway there is, entrepreneurship is often referred to as a career choice, but entrepreneurship is a lifestyle. Your lifestyle affects what happens in business, just like it affects what happens at home. When you're doing really well in business, it's going to affect what's happening at home. Your kids go to a better school, you buy your spouse a better house, you travel the world.

Entrepreneurship is a lifestyle. If you're not prepared to accept what comes along with that lifestyle, then maybe entrepreneurship is not some-

> "I love it when people doubt me. It makes me work harder to prove them wrong."
>
> **Derek Jeter**

thing for you. Entrepreneurship comes with ups and downs and challenges, and it also comes with this responsibility to others and this responsibility for others.

TREVOR OTT'S FIVE SUCCESS & WEALTH TIPS

1. **Stop looking for a return on investment.** Number one policy. Return on investment is really a term for the investment market. And it's not necessarily a term that should be applied in all areas. Often times, the number one thing entrepreneurs are looking for is a return on investment. That's a bit of a gamble. So I put $100 in and I want to get $1,000 out. What I want you to know is all success and all returns don't have dollar signs on them.

2. **Learn to appreciate the highest form of a return.** The highest form of a return is a return on finishing. When I think of finishing, I mean finishing something to the point that it can go on without your on-site supervision. Many of us have not finished. That's why we're not profitable. I'll give you an example of somebody who finished. Steve Jobs is no longer alive. But how do we know that he finished? Did his company die? No!

His company is more profitable now than it was then. That's because he finished, and you're seeing the return on what he finished. Here's the thing, though—there are many people who make money and never finish. But there are very few people who finish and don't make money.

So, if you finish something, you have a higher chance of generating revenue. But if you don't finish here's what happens: any results you produce are unsustainable. So you made some money? Because you didn't put a process in place, you can't maintain the result. You have to learn to finish because finishing is a learned behavior. Finishing ain't easy, folks.

3. **Invest in the Genesis of your success.** Anybody involved in any type of investing, you know the earlier you get in, the bigger profits you will reap. For some of us, we're waiting for someone else to invest in our success. Don't wait! Invest your beliefs, invest your time, your resources and your efforts.

I wish I could have been back in the 1980s, been one of those Microsoft millionaires, those who invested in Microsoft in the very beginning. Heck, I wish I would have got Apple when it was a dollar a share—how much money would I have now? Those people got in early. But I can't do that. However, I can invest in my own dreams right now.

You need to invest in yourself; you need to be first. You need to invest in the Genesis of your success. Maybe that's investing in a web program or branding company, or copywriter or graphic artist, maybe it's investing in a coach, or a mentor or a trainer. I'm not talking about dollars and cents, folks. I'm really talking about investing in the resources that will take your business to the next level.

4. **Learn to sell the vision and position the product.** Help others see what you see for them. Too many times as entre-

preneurs we spend too much time trying to sell the product. The thing is, the person doesn't necessarily understand why you want them to have the product.

Look at a Weight Watchers commercial. They don't show you the special health bars or the WW meals; what they show you is this woman or this guy who was overweight, and now is thin and having a better life. They are helping you see what they see; what they see is a healthier life. What they see is that mother whose daughter couldn't put her arms around her. And now, eight months later, her daughter can actually put her arms all the way around her. They helped you see what they see for you.

After they helped you see the vision, then you buy into the vision. The first thing you buy is the vision. And then they position the product as the way for you to achieve your dream and your goals. You basically buy the product, which is the second thing you buy, and the way of achieving your goals, as opposed to the company achieving their goals.

Your goal is very simple. You want to sell a product. But their goal is also very simple; they want to know, what's in it for me? Sell the vision and position the product.

5. **Understand that there's a difference between a purchase and an investment.** A purchase is this: somebody's buying something, like a cost. People ask me all the time,

what's does this cost? I say there is no cost. It's an invest-ment. Ok, what do you mean by that?

Sales is merely the opportunity to invest in themselves (or their business) through the products and services that you offer. How much does one of your products cost? Nothing! It is an investment, and you are offering the person to in-vest in your products and services through the investment in the product and services that you offer. That is very im-portant.

Last but not least, remember this: learn to create a bond with the client first. The business definition of a bond is a trust highway over which commerce can be transacted. Learn to create a bond with the client. If you don't have a bond, it's always going to be painful to do any type of transaction, whether it be an investment transaction, it doesn't matter. It's always going to be hard because there's no bond. Create the bond first.

Notes From The Publisher:
"50 Shades Of Publishing"

I hope you have enjoyed this book and apply the tips that have made these authors, contributors and leaders more abundant. Barrett Matthews is a 'Power of One' leader and thinker. He is the 'Perfect' example of how a book can change a leader's life.

Everyone has a story, but very few people share it and tell it in a way that could create abundance and a legacy. The authors in this book have an opportunity to not only share their gold nuggets, but to connect with you, the reader.

This connection is also to each other! Every time one author gives away or sells a book, he or she has made a difference in the other author's lives by introducing them to a new reader. This is a big reason the book '50 Shades of Wealth: The Allure Of Success' is a big success and will be an even bigger success as a series. If you want to know why this series could change your life, there is a diagram titled 'Social Proof Viral Campaign' which explains the power of having a marketing plan that is robust enough to give each author tens of thousands of dollars in exposure.

Imagine this book going to hundreds of events because the publisher is a sponsor and connected to a marketing company that does over a thousand events a year. Each time this book is featured at an event and the book goes viral on social media, it is giving tremendous exposure to the book and the authors involved.

Every time the book is photographed with other books in the publishing program, all the books are tagged with the authors which further breaks algorithms and again the authors and the book(s) go viral at almost zero cost to the author. Why is this important? In business, when you are a guru and the expense of the public learning you are a guru is negligible, then you are getting a high return for a small investment in being an author in a book.

Most authors don't experience this because they choose to self publish and don't have a marketing system and access to huge events that will show off their book. So what inevitably happens is the book becomes a secret and worse the author gets discouraged and never writes another book. This is totally avoidable with the help of a publishing company with a strength in marketing, promotion and social media. Refer to chart 'Self Publishing vs. Perfect Publishing vs. Traditional Publishing'

Here is some crazy math for you to think about:
- 81% of people want to write a book
- 1% actually do it
- Of that 1% almost all of them lose money on their investment because they don't market the book, so over 90% of them never write another book and worse they either store what they believed would sell or they didn't order very many because they didn't believe their marketing would get them book sales.

This does not have to be the experience you have when you publish. I assure you Barrett Matthews is a 'Perfect' example of how a person should approach publishing. He met with Perfect Publishing, he followed a marketing game plan and communicated his moves and supported our PR company (The Umbrella Syndicate) to get him exposure when he was either attending big events or producing them himself. He is obviously the organizer of this book and since it is about creating wealth, and this book will make all of his contributors wealthier because they are connected to a marketing system that uses a 'Social Proof Viral Campaign' that is as efficient as anyone could ask for or imagine.

Ken Rochon

Self-Publishing Vanity Publishing	Perfect Publishing	Traditional Publishing
Benefits	**Benefits**	**Benefits**
Complete Control	Complete Control	Experience
Profits per Book High	Excellent Distribution	Excellent Distribution
Rights to Book	Experience	Good Marketing
	Robust Marketing Campaign	Team
Problems	Mentorship	**Problems**
Low Distribution	Profits per Book High	No Control
Weak Marketing	Rights to Book	Profits per Book Low
High Chance of Mistakes	Best Social Media Campaign	Weak Social Media
Weak Social Media		Lose Rights to Book

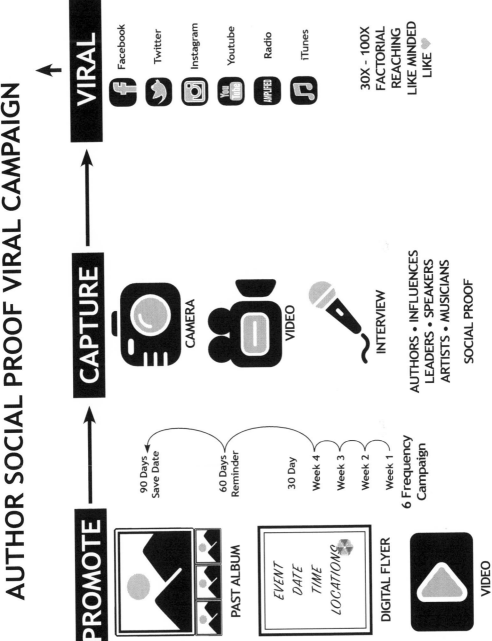

AUTHOR SOCIAL PROOF VIRAL CAMPAIGN

PROMOTE

PAST ALBUM

EVENT
DATE
TIME
LOCATIONS

DIGITAL FLYER

VIDEO

90 Days Save Date
60 Days Reminder
30 Day
Week 4
Week 3
Week 2
Week 1

6 Frequency Campaign

CAPTURE

CAMERA

VIDEO

INTERVIEW

AUTHORS • INFLUENCES
LEADERS • SPEAKERS
ARTISTS • MUSICIANS

SOCIAL PROOF

VIRAL

Facebook
Twitter
Instagram
Youtube
Radio
iTunes

30X - 100X
FACTORIAL
REACHING
LIKE MINDED
LIKE ♥

ABOUT THE AUTHOR

 Barrett Matthews is an amazing author, speaker, trainer, and productivity expert. Known as the "Get It Done Coach", "The Excuse Killer", and "The Idea Man", Barrett has shared his unique brand of productivity genius with companies like Metro Public Adjustment, Peak Performers Institute, and FraserNet. Barrett is committed to showing individuals how to start and grow any business, with any product, and any service, on any budget with his creative insight and unique way of seeing the larger picture.

Barrett is the author of *Why Didn't You Get It Done?* and co-author of *Congratulations, You Just Lost Your Job.* With this powerhouse effort of *50 Shades of Wealth: The Allure Of Success,* Barrett Matthews has embarked upon a brilliant series that will inspire and empower many to success.

As a dynamic speaker and coach, Barrett has been a force behind moving people to Get It Done in several arenas. He is constantly being asked to speak and inspire greatness with individuals and organizations. As you read *50 Shades Of Wealth: The Allure Of Success,* consider the person who is able to pull together such genius to collaborate in this masterpiece. To have Barrett Matthews pour his knowledge into you or your team, simply text SPEAK to 929-244-4323 and find his availability to come to you.

More Books From

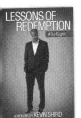   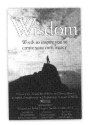 

  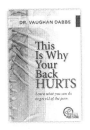  

    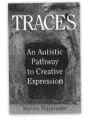

   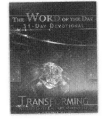 

Your Book Here

www.PerfectPublishing.me

Made in the USA
Columbia, SC
31 March 2018